A TRANSACTIONAL MATTER: A GUIDE TO BUSINESS LAWYERING

BRIAN K. KRUMM

GEORGE W. KUNEY

DONNA C. LOOPER

The University of Tennessee College of Law

WEST
ACADEMIC
PUBLISHING

© 2017 LEG, Inc. d/b/a West Academic
      444 Cedar Street, Suite 700
      St. Paul, MN 55101
      1-877-888-1330

West, West Academic Publishing, and West Academic are trademarks of West Publishing Corporation, used under license.

Printed in the United States of America

ISBN: 978-0-314-28908-7

ACKNOWLEDGMENTS

The authors thank the following University of Tennessee Business Law Clinic student attorneys who worked on the iCare transactional matter: lead counsel Caleb Barron, Ashley Jenks, Rachel Lokitz, Hannah Lowe, and Alan Moore, as well as Daniel Browning, Maurice Antoine Echols, Jonathon Edwards, Yousuf Malik, Jonathon Thomaston, Lin Ye, and April Candace Young.

The authors thank Christopher Coleman and Elizabeth Holland, UT College of Law Class of 2018, for their significant contribution of time and detail-oriented effort to this project, the manuscript, and its supporting documentation.

ABOUT THE AUTHORS

Brian K. Krumm received his B.A. from the State University of New York at Oswego, his M.P.A. from the Maxwell School at Syracuse University, and his J.D. from the University of Tennessee College of Law. Prior to law school Brian worked with Booz Allen Hamilton Management Consultants in New York City and Washington, D.C., where he was engaged in both domestic and international client assignments. Krumm later held senior management positions in the Office of the General Manager and Office of Finance with the Tennessee Valley Authority. After law school, Brian primarily focused his practice on the representation of small- and medium-sized business clients, on matters of corporate governance, preparation of transactional documents, and business litigation. Brian has also served in Tennessee state government as Assistant Commissioner of Employment Security, Deputy Commissioner of Labor, and as Policy Advisor to the Governor. At The University of Tennessee College of Law in Knoxville, Tennessee He teaches the Business Law and Trademark Clinic courses. He is admitted to practice in Tennessee.

George W. Kuney is a Lindsay Young Distinguished Professor of Law and Director of the Clayton Center for Entrepreneurial Law and the LL.M. in United States Business Law at The University of Tennessee College of Law. He holds a J.D. from the University of California, Hastings

College of the Law, an M.B.A. from The University of San Diego, and a B.A. in Economics from the University of California, Santa Cruz. Before joining the UT faculty in 2000, he was a partner in the Allen Matkins firm's San Diego office. Previously he practiced with the Howard Rice and Morrison & Foerster firms in his hometown of San Francisco, doing litigation and transactional work largely in the context of business restructuring and insolvency. He teaches business law courses including Business Associations, Contracts, Contract Drafting, Commercial Leasing, Commercial Law, Consumer Bankruptcy, Debtor-Creditor, Mergers and Acquisitions, Representing Enterprises, and Workouts and Reorganizations. Kuney writes books and articles about business, contracts, commercial law, and insolvency-related topics. He also advises clients, consults, and serves as an expert witness regarding bankruptcy, contracts, agency and corporate law, restructuring, reorganization, and related subjects. He is admitted to practice law in both California and Tennessee.

Donna C. Looper is an Adjunct Professor of Law at The University of Tennessee College of Law where she teaches Legal Process. She received her J.D. from the University of California, Hastings College of the Law and her A.B. from Barnard College, Columbia University. She clerked for the Chief Judge of the United States District Court for the Eastern District of Louisiana and then for the United States Court of Appeals for the Ninth Circuit. Before teaching at the University of Tennessee College of Law, Ms. Looper was a Senior Attorney for the California Court of

Appeal, Fourth District, Division One and, prior to that, was in private practice in San Diego and San Francisco. She is admitted to practice law in both California and Tennessee and consults in matters nationwide.

ALSO BY THE AUTHORS

Krumm & Kuney:

THE ENTREPRENEURIAL LAW CLINIC HANDBOOK (West 2012).

Kuney:

CONTRACTS: TRANSACTIONS AND LITIGATION (4th ed., Thompson/West 2017, with Robert M. Lloyd).

EXPERIENCING REMEDIES (West 2015).

BANKRUPTCY IN PRACTICE (5th ed. ABI 2015, with Michael L. Bernstein).

BUSINESS REORGANIZATIONS (3rd ed. Lexis 2013, with Michael Gerber and Edward Janger).

JUDGMENT ENFORCEMENT IN TENNESSEE (Amazon/Center for Entrepreneurial Law 2013, with Wendy G. Patrick).

BAMBOOZLED? ANATOMY OF A BANKRUPTCY: BAYSTATE V. BOWERS AND ITS AFTERMATH (West 2012).

CONTRACTS: TRANSACTIONS AND LITIGATION (3rd ed., Thompson/West 2011, with Robert M. Lloyd).

THE ELEMENTS OF CONTRACT DRAFTING WITH QUESTIONS AND CLAUSES FOR CONSIDERATION (3rd ed., Thompson/West 2011).

SALES, NEGOTIABLE INSTRUMENTS, AND PAYMENT SYSTEMS: UCC ARTICLES 2, 3, 4, AND 5 (Center for Entrepreneurial Law 2010, with Robert M. Lloyd).

SECURED TRANSACTIONS: UCC ARTICLE 9 AND BANKRUPTCY (Center for Entrepreneurial Law 2009, with Robert M. Lloyd).

MASTERING BANKRUPTCY LAW (Carolina Academic Press 2008).

CHAPTER 11–101: THE ESSENTIALS OF CHAPTER 11 PRACTICE (ABI 2007, with Jonathan P. Friedland, Michael L. Bernstein, and Professor John D. Ayer).

Kuney & Looper:

A CRIMINAL MATTER (forthcoming).

LEGAL DRAFTING IN A NUTSHELL (4th ed. West 2017).

LEGAL DRAFTING PROCESS, TECHNIQUES, AND EXERCISES (3d ed. West 2017).

A CIVIL MATTER (West 2014).

MASTERING APPELLATE ADVOCACY AND PROCESS (Rev. Printing, Carolina Academic Press 2015).

MASTERING INTELLECTUAL PROPERTY LAW (Carolina Academic Press 2008).

MASTERING LEGAL ANALYSIS AND DRAFTING (Carolina Academic Press 2009).

OUTLINE

A
TRANSACTIONAL
MATTER:
A GUIDE TO
BUSINESS
LAWYERING

INTRODUCTION

Law students and the public have a basic understanding of what goes on in a litigation-based legal practice, especially criminal litigation, based upon books, movies, and television. But there is another side to the practice of law that is generally out of sight: transactional practice. Apparently less prone to dramatization, transactional practice is actually a much larger proportion of the practice of law than litigation. Some estimates of the proportion of U.S. lawyers that are engaged in transactional or regulatory practice run to over 75%. Introductory or overview materials describing the transactional side of law practice have historically been scarce. This book aims to help fill that void by detailing a series of transactions involving the formation and sale of a business that were undertaken by law students and their supervising professor at The University of Tennessee College of Law. In detailing and documenting this process, the book introduces readers to contract law, secured transactions, corporate law, finance, employment law, tort law, and intellectual property law in an applied setting. A Transactional Matter describes the transactional legal work necessary to form a business entity, enter into agreements necessary for its operation, and enable the founders to derive profit from their labor and their invention. It chronicles how the founders of a small, University-based software venture named "iCare" set out to commercialize the intellectual property they developed as part of their research efforts and the role of their legal counsel—student attorneys and their supervising professor—in assisting them in that process.

The purpose of this book is to take the reader through the basic business and legal steps involved with forming a company, licensing technology, developing that technology, and harvesting or monetizing the assets that the business created. Hopefully, it will demystify the process involved. Although iCare was a short-lived company, all the transactions described here and the transactional documents and instruments involved in this transaction are applicable to deals involving companies as large as Google (Alphabet), Apple Computer, Berkshire Hathaway, and Amgen Pharmaceuticals. We hope that this discussion and presentation will pique your interest in business lawyering, especially as the majority of practicing lawyers in the United States are not primarily courtroom lawyers or litigators but, rather, function as business deal or regulatory attorneys, fulfilling the role of trusted advisor to their clients as they navigate the seas of business and commerce.

The book begins by explaining how the new entrepreneurs went about choosing the form of business entity they initially adopted to provide the proper management and governance of the enterprise. This includes taking account of their risk assessment and desire to limit liability, analyzing their short and long term capital needs, and accounting for their future tax considerations. It progresses to describe the growth of the company in terms of retaining a Chief Operating Officer (COO) to oversee the management of day-to-day operations of the firm, entering into a licensing agreement for the intellectual property, obtaining financing for operations, and beta-testing the prototype software. The book then discusses the process that the company undertook when third parties became interested in purchasing the software to enhance their own business objectives, allowing the company and its owners to "harvest" or "monetize" the fruits of their labors. This includes the use of non-disclosure agreements to protect the company's interests during the negotiation process, entering into the letter of intent that provided the initial framework for the transaction under which the business was sold to a third party, and, subsequently, the negotiation and preparation of all the documents that are part of the Asset Purchase Agreement.

This book makes use of hyperlinks in the e-book version, and is supported by a website (url: http://www.kuneylooperacivilmatter.com/) containing all of the documents and authorities discussed keyed to [x] references for the print version, in order to allow the reader to access the documents that were used to memorialize the various business transactions entered into along the way, as well as the documents that became a part of the Asset Purchase Agreement. To make the best instructional use of this book, the reader should use the links to examine the source documents to gain an understanding of the legal concepts and techniques used to support the underlying business objectives and transactions. At the end of each chapter, questions are posed to assist the reader in gaining a deeper understanding of the context and content of how the various documents were used to support the underlying business transactions. If you are reading this book in a class at school, it is highly likely that not everyone in your class will do this. *Be one that does*. It will enhance your understanding of transactional law practice.

CHAPTER 1

FORMATION OF THE BUSINESS

I. THE ENTREPRENEURS AND THEIR INNOVATION: "ICARE"—A CLINICAL SIMULATION TOOL FOR EDUCATING HEALTH CARE PROFESSIONALS IN THE USE OF ELECTRONIC HEALTH RECORDS SYSTEMS

Health care information technology is essential in supporting the transformation and improvement of health care in America. Critical to this transformation is the use of electronic health record (EHR) systems. However, until recently, nurses and medical professionals were essentially completely untrained in using EHR systems. In early 2008, Professor Tami Wyatt and her graduate student Mathew Bell at the University of Tennessee College of Nursing began researching existing applications and software used to educate nursing students on the use of Electronic Health Records (EHR) systems. In most hospitals and other medical facilities around the country, a patient's medical record is entered into a computer as an EHR. In most cases, only licensed/certified practitioners are allowed to enter patient information into an EHR. Although a majority of nursing students are exposed to EHRs during their clinical training, in most cases they are not given the opportunity to document care electronically within them. However, upon graduation and licensure, nurses are often expected to document their care electronically on their first clinical day on the job.

The nursing program was having difficulty giving students experiences using health information technology, so they conducted research for systems to use in their simulation lab. Unfortunately, some of these systems cost up to $70,000 per year. Because that cost was prohibitive, Wyatt and Bell embarked on designing the parameters to develop their own system for educating students in using health information technology and EHRs. Once the functional system design was completed, they contacted Xueping Li and Chayawat Indranoi of the University's College of Engineering (Industrial & Information Engineering) for assistance with developing a database and software program based on the system design. After the database and software development were completed in early 2009, they were tested in the College of Nursing and Wyatt and Bell disclosed the innovation to the University's Office of Technology Transfer ("UTRF") as required by University policy.

The newly developed system that the team called "iCare" [81] would allow students to learn about EHR systems within the framework of their current educational curriculum both in the classroom and simulation environments. iCare was designed to mirror the functionality of currently used EHRs with educational tools built into the documentation experience. Specifically, when working on a simulated patient-care problem, nursing students could electronically document their simulated care using iCare. Additionally nursing students could record and retrieve data pertinent to that care, such as physical assessments, vital signs, and medication administration. They could also retrieve physician orders and diagnostic results for the patient-care scenarios built into the iCare software program. Nursing faculty could build their own patient-care scenarios and would then be afforded the opportunity to evaluate their students on their respective documentation of physical assessments as well as general EHR documentation skills. Thus, the iCare academic EHR clinical simulation tool was born.

The University of Tennessee is the owner of any intellectual property ("IP") developed by University employees during the course of their employment or developed by anyone using university facilities, or funds, with the exception of books and scholarly articles. This applies to all faculty, staff, and student employees. Once the intellectual property is disclosed to the University, the University will transfer ownership to University of Tennessee Research Foundation ("UTRF") for management and protection of the invention. UTRF is a 501(c)(3) nonprofit corporation formed to protect, manage, and commercialize intellectual property created at the University. Once the invention is disclosed to UTRF, a licensing associate is assigned to assess the invention's commercial viability and determine whether the invention should be protected through patent, copyright, or trade secret law.

Recognizing the potential educational value that the new EHR system, iCare, provided to students at the University of Tennessee College of Nursing, Wyatt and Bell envisioned expanding the use of this system to other health professional education programs like pharmacy and physical therapy— programs that must also ensure their graduates' competence in data entry, retrieval, and management of healthcare records. As a result, the team decided to form a company to take their product to the national market. They discussed this idea with UTRF and were given assurances that if they formed a company, UT could grant it an Intellectual Property License [1] to use the technology they had developed in exchange for royalties from any sales that the new system might generate.

II. INITIAL BUSINESS FORMATION

A. DECIDING ON THE TYPE OF BUSINESS ENTITY

Wyatt and Bell then sought the advice of an attorney who could assist them in creating an appropriate business entity for the proposed new venture. They met with a private attorney who discussed with them the various factors that should be considered in forming a business entity such as:

- The nature and goals of the business

- The proper management and governance of the enterprise

- Determining risks and limiting liability

- Analyzing short and long term capital needs

- Providing for continuity of the entity

- Tax considerations

After discussing these factors and consulting an accountant, Wyatt and Bell decided that a director-managed limited liability company [2] would be the best business entity to meet their anticipated needs. Although they believed they had a great product that could be used in health-care-related educational programs across the country, they had no experience forming and running a business. They anticipated that they would have to hire someone to run the business for them. That person could then help them build the business to the point where it could be sold to a company that already had a presence in the health care information management marketplace.[1] However, in the meantime the team of inventors or "founders"—Wyatt, Bell, Li, and Indranoi—all wanted to share equally in the decision-making concerning the new venture and share equally in any profits which were derived from the business. They did not want the person they hired to be part of the group of initial owners.

---

[1]   This is what is known in the business world as an "exit strategy." Other possible exit strategies include taking the company public in an initial public offering, or shutting it down—liquidating it—once its purpose has been fulfilled. Thinking through an exit strategy at the inception of a venture is an important step in determining the proper structure of the business entity and its relationships with the founders, officers, directors, employees, and consultants. If clients are not focused on potential exit strategies, good business lawyers will raise the issue and pursue it to its conclusion early on in their discussions with the client.

A limited liability company (or "LLC") offered the founders a form of business entity that limited personal non-tax liability for:

- contracts such as leases and service agreements;

- long-term debt (owed to banks, financial institutions, and individual debt investors);

- short-term debt owed to creditors on accounts; and

- torts to third parties.

This limited liability is based upon the law's recognition that a properly formed LLC, like a properly formed corporation, is an entity separate from the founders and those that work for it. So, if the LLC breaches a contract, the LLC is liable, but, for instance, the founders that created the LLC are not, unless they were parties to the contract in their individual capacity, such as when they guarantee or "co-sign" a loan. There are exceptions to this rule of non-liability, mostly rooted in misbehavior and inequitable treatment that makes it unjust to allow the members or shareholders to enjoy this limited liability, but the legal bar that must be cleared prior to disregarding the LLC or corporate form is a very high one.[2]

---

[2] From an investor's point of view, this limited liability is necessary in order to induce them to invest. Think of it this way: would you want to invest, say, $20,000 in a company, becoming a shareholder or member, if that meant that when the company did something that led to liability, you could be found liable for more than your initial investment? Imagine how many people would be

In addition to limiting personal liability, the founders were also concerned about how any income produced by the business entity would be taxed by both the state and federal governments. With regard to federal income tax, IRS so-called "check-the-box" provisions allow unincorporated businesses,[3] like an

---

unwilling to invest in oil companies because they could be wiped out financially if the company blew a well head that dumped oil all over the Alaskan or the Gulf shore. With the corporate or LLC form of entity, you are protected from that (subject to the exception described above), and thus encouraged to invest your capital or other assets in a business, which is thought to be good in our society. But do not get carried away with this notion of limited liability. Remember—you are always liable for your own acts. So, if you form an LLC and serve as its officer and, in the course of your duties as officer, you injure someone by, say, running them down in your car, they have a right to sue you *and* the LLC to recover. The same applies to contracts that you sign in your individual capacity, like personal guaranty of a loan to the LLC that you guarantee.

[3]   An unincorporated business entity is really any business entity that is not a "corporation" established under state law that has filed a charter with the Secretary of State and has written by-laws that establish the rights and duties of the directors, officers, and shareholders. If businesses incorporate, the owners will have to decide what sort of corporation the business will be for IRS [3] purposes. Businesses need not be a C corporation [4]. It is possible to be an S corporation [5] and avoid double taxation altogether while still enjoying the limited liability that incorporation provides. Federal income tax laws allow for the S corporation as a means of encouraging small business development. The S corporation is a corporation that elects to be taxed under subchapter S (rather than subchapter C) of the Internal Revenue Code [6]. For the most part, the S corporation passes its income, losses, deductions, and credits through to its shareholders for inclusion on their individual tax returns, as if the business were a partnership, and its income is taxed at the individual rate instead of the corporate rate. Therefore, in many cases, shareholders benefit during the early years of a business, when losses are likely and can offset other shareholder income, and earnings avoid double taxation. There are limitations on the ability of

LLC, with two or more members to be taxed either as partnerships or corporations. If an entity is taxed as a partnership, then the entity does not pay any income tax as an entity. Rather, when monies are disbursed from the entity to the partners, they are known as partnership distributions or "draws" and they are included in the individual partners' income, which is taxed at the individual level. On the other hand, when an entity is taxed as a corporation, then the corporation's earnings are taxed at the entity level and any distributions to shareholders are taxed at the individual level. This is what is known as "double taxation" of corporate earnings. It results from the internal revenue code's recognition of the particular business entity as a separate taxpayer.

Unincorporated businesses with two or more members are automatically taxed as partnerships unless they elect to be taxed as corporations by making an entity classification election on IRS Form 8832—the form for the "check-the-box" election. With

---

shareholders to deduct losses of S corporations, partnerships, and LLCs. To be eligible for S corporation treatment, the corporation must:

- be a domestic corporation with only one class of stock with identical rights to operating and liquidating distributions, although different voting rights are permissible;

- have no more than 100 shareholders, all of whom must be individuals or certain trusts or estates;

- have only citizens or legal residents of the U.S. as shareholders; and

- gain the agreement of all its shareholders.

Brian K. Krumm & George W. Kuney, THE ENTREPRENEURIAL LAW HANDBOOK 37 (2012).

the understanding that it might be some time before they realized any profit from the fledgling business, the iCare founders chose to be taxed as a partnership, allowing the founders to allocate profits and losses of the LLC directly to their personal income tax statements.

Although the LLC is not itself subject to federal income tax, the LLC must file an informational income tax return with the IRS, using IRS form 1065. On form 1065, the LLC reports both its taxable income and how those earnings are allocated to each member using Schedule K-1, a copy of which is furnished to each member for use in preparing the member's personal income tax return. Taxable income generated by the LLC is taxed only once for federal income tax purposes, at the member level. Each member's personal federal income tax return will show the member's share of taxable income or loss (although the member's ability to deduct any losses may be limited). Accordingly, each partner is responsible for the associated taxes on that member's allocated share of the LLC income (whether or not the LLC actually distributes funds to the member).

The founders also were informed that many states tax business entities that have limited liability differently than they tax those which do not provide such protection. However, after consulting with their accountant, they did not feel that this was an important factor since they did not anticipate any immediate income production from the venture. The founders went away from the initial consultation with their attorney believing that they were now operating as iCare Academics, LLC, doing business as iCare.

B.   ENGAGING THE UNIVERSITY OF TENNESSEE COLLEGE OF LAW BUSINESS LAW CLINIC

Since the founders had their own full-time academic jobs and responsibilities, the next task at hand was to hire someone to assist them with developing a business plan and managing the day-to-day activities of the business. They consulted with a local entrepreneurial business development organization, associated with the University's College of Business, for advice on how to go about hiring such an individual. A team of advisors was put together as an outside advisory board that had experience in assisting small businesses succeed in business development and bringing new products to market. Because the advisors needed to know details about both the business strategy and intellectual property that iCare possessed, one of the business advisors recommended that each of the advisors sign a confidentiality and non-disclosure agreement [7]—colloquially known as an "NDA"—to protect the company from any unauthorized disclosure or use of company sensitive information.

After interviewing a number of individuals and negotiating the terms of employment, Wyatt and Bell spoke with another attorney that was recommended by the advisory board, Professor Brian Krumm at the University of Tennessee College of Law Business

Law Clinic,[4] to help them with drafting an
employment agreement which defined the roles,

---

[4]   In the UT College of Law Business Law Clinic, third-year
law students, working under the close supervision of a full-time
law professor with transactional experience, represent the
business clients. Students in the clinic have the opportunity to
acquire skills, training, and experience essential to working
successfully with business clients and thus, to bridge the gap
between law school and the practice of law. Under the rules of the
Supreme Court of Tennessee students in the UT College of Law
Business Law Clinic are allowed to practice law under supervision
of the full-time law professor, and thus are referred to as "student
attorneys."

The Business Law Clinic is modeled after the structure of a
transactional law firm and provides legal advice to businesses in
the following critical areas:

- Business planning;
- Entity selection and registration;
- State and local business licenses;
- Federal, state, and local tax issues;
- Financing documentation and securities issues;
- Leases and other commercial contracts;
- Employment agreements;
- Trademark and copyright registration, IP licensing
  agreements, and material transfer and non-disclosure
  agreements;
- IP counseling regarding branding, copyrights,
  trademarks, trade secrets, freedom to operate, unfair
  competition, antitrust, publicity rights, and privacy
  rights.

Through this model, the Business Law Clinic, in conjunction with
the Anderson Center for Entrepreneurship and Innovation at the
UT College of Business Administration, is one of the cornerstones
of the innovation ecosystem in the Knoxville area.

Before enrolling in the Business Law Clinic, students must
have taken Fundamental Concepts of Income Taxation,
Introduction to Business Transactions, Business Associations, and
Income Taxation of Business Organizations and must have taken
or be taking Legal Profession and Contract Drafting. The Business

responsibilities, and compensation for the position they were calling Chief Operating Officer (COO).

As a preliminary matter, Krumm assigned two student attorneys to interview Wyatt and Bell to get a fuller understanding of the matter.[5] As part of the interview, they asked for a copy of iCare's articles of organization [2] and operating agreement so they could determine what steps needed to be taken in order for iCare to effectively enter into an employment agreement with the new COO. When Wyatt and Bell said they didn't know what those documents were, the student attorneys searched the

---

Law Clinic is a six-credit course, normally offered during the fall and spring semesters.

[5]　Client/matter intake is very important in the legal profession. Unlike almost any other profession, the first initial interview must include a conflict check to make sure that the lawyer or firm does and has not represented parties that are averse to the new potential client. This is accomplished by interviewing the potential client and having them disclose all adverse and potentially adverse parties. The lawyer or firm then checks its records of prior and ongoing representations to determine if a conflict exists. If one is identified, a waiver may be sought from the adverse party. Alternatively, if the conflict is determined to be actual and ongoing, the prospective client's matter cannot be taken on and the potential client should be informed of this non-representation clearly and in writing. Assuming the matter clears the conflict check process, it is wise to formalize the representation with an agreement, often in the form of a letter agreement signed by the attorney and the client, that delineates clearly the scope of the representation, the fees and costs, if any, to be had by the client and the firm, the manner in which the representation can be terminated by either or both the firm and the client, and the mutual understandings and responsibilities of both parties. Relying on vague understandings of the existence and scope of the attorney-client representation is a recipe for disagreement, dissension, dissatisfaction, and malpractice claims.

Tennessee Secretary of State's database[6] and found that articles of organization had not been filed for iCare Academics LLC. Although articles of organization had been prepared for iCare LLC on August 19, 2009, they were never filed, *which meant that no LLC had been formed.* When business people act together and do not form a separate entity to house the business, Tennessee law's default—and that of many other jurisdictions—is to find that they are partners in a general partnership. As a result, Wyatt and Bell were dismayed to learn that, because their prior attorney had not filed the formation documents, they were operating as a partnership. This meant that each of them was jointly and severally liable for all of the obligations of the business entity incurred to date.

Confused and unhappy with this state of affairs, they asked the student attorneys what needed to be done to fix this situation. Consequently, the founders entered into a retention agreement [9] with the Business Law Clinic that included formation of the business as well as software licensing. The student attorneys advised them that they would prepare the articles of organization and operating agreement but needed to ask more questions to determine how to best prepare these documents.[7]

---

[6]   *Business Entity Detail-Academic Technology Innovations,* TENN. SECRETARY OF ST., Business Information Search [10] (search "iCare"; then follow "000615979" hyperlink).

[7]   This mix up between what the founders thought their first attorney was going to do following their consultation points to the importance of using clear and comprehensive engagement letters and other documentation of what work is expected, desired, and

C. STEPS TAKEN IN FORMING ICARE ACADEMIC LLC

1. The Articles of Organization

In order for an LLC to come into existence, articles of organization must be prepared and filed with the Secretary of State in the state in which the LLC is formed. An LLC's articles of organization are the highest-level governing documentation for the entity, and thus the most difficult to change, like the U.S. Constitution is for the federal government. After some discussion with the student attorneys, Wyatt and Bell decided that it was not cost effective to form the LLC in a jurisdiction outside of iCare's home state of Tennessee. Obtaining limited liability in the state where the business is physically located is called home-state incorporation (even though the business, in this instance, is an LLC and not a corporation). Some business owners think that they will save money by incorporating in a state with low fees, even if their company is neither located nor conducts business in that state. This is often a mistake. In iCare Academic's case, the founders determined that the added costs of fulfilling the ongoing taxation and reporting requirements imposed by another state of incorporation

---

undertaken in the attorney-client relationship. Failure to ensure clear, mutual expectations is a recipe for unhappy clients, disputes, and malpractice claims against the attorneys involved.

outweighed the perceived benefits of incorporating outside the home-state.[8]

In Tennessee, articles of organization for LLCs are governed by Tenn. Code Ann. § 48–249–202 [17]. This statute requires articles of organization to, *among other things*, set out the name of the LLC, the addresses of its initial registered office and its principal executive office, and to state whether the

---

[8] When selecting the jurisdiction in which to create a business entity, keep in mind that cost, taxation, and laws vary from state to state, making some states advantageous for certain small business owners. No matter if the business is a C corporation, S corporation, LLC, limited liability partnership (a "LLP"), limited partnership (a "LP"), or nonprofit corporation, filing fees must be paid to the state when incorporation documents are filed. The entity will be subject to ongoing requirements and fees imposed by that state. Many states also have filing requirements for individuals (sole proprietorships and partnerships) that are doing business under an assumed name, requiring a filing for a certificate for a fictitious or assumed name. Some business owners mistakenly think they will save money by incorporating in a state with low fees, even if their company is neither located nor conducts business in that state. Keep in mind that companies incorporated in one state but doing business in other states still must register or qualify to transact business in those states. When deciding a company's state of incorporation, business owners or their attorneys should research those states' statutes to determine if there are advantages. Consider how sole proprietorships, partnerships, and limited liability entities are taxed by each state and the taxation requirements imposed on foreign-qualified businesses, if foreign qualification is necessary. Does a state impose an income tax on corporations and LLCs? Does it have a minimum tax or a franchise tax? The added costs of fulfilling the ongoing taxation requirements imposed by the state of incorporation and state(s) of foreign qualification often outweigh the perceived benefits of incorporating outside the home state. Try calculating the company's projected revenue for its first few years of existence and then evaluate states in terms of the true amount of taxes required, to see if there may be an advantage.

LLC is member-managed, manager-managed, or director-managed. The founders had decided to name the LLC "iCare Academic Limited Liability Company" and that it would be director-managed. The initial members and directors of the LLC were the four founders, Tami Wyatt, Matthew Bell, Xueping Li, and Chayawat Indranoi.

The next item that needed to be determined was iCare Academic's registered agent for service of process and its office location. The purpose of the registered agent is to provide a legal address within the state where the LLC can be served with a summons and complaint or other legal documents in the event of a legal action or lawsuit. The registered agent is also the person to whom the state government sends all official documents required each year for tax and legal purposes, such as franchise tax notices and annual report forms. The founders had decided to rent office space at a local business incubator, which provided an array of support services included in the rent, so that address would be used for the registered office. Thus, it would seem only logical that the registered agent should be the COO since that individual would be handling the day to day operations of the business. However, until iCare Academic was properly formed and was able to officially enter into an employment agreement with the COO, they decided that Bell would serve as registered agent at his home address, and that a change of registered office and agent would be made once the COO was hired.

The student attorneys also advised the founders that they should include indemnification and exculpation provisions in the articles of organization. *Indemnification* is an act—here an agreement—to compensate someone for damage, loss, or injury.[9] *Exculpation* is an act—here a payment—to clear someone of blame or financial responsibility for something. Both provisions are commonly placed in an LLC's articles of organization. The indemnification provision would allow the LLC to pay for damages for any claim that was brought against a member, manager, employee, or agent of the LLC for any acts or omissions in their official capacity. The exculpation provision would protect the members from liability for breaches of their fiduciary duties to the entity and other members that did not arise to the level of bad faith.[10] These provisions

---

[9]   *See generally* George W. Kuney, The Elements of Contract Drafting: With Questions and Clauses for Consideration 101 (4th ed. 2014). [11]

[10]   The scope of indemnification and exculpation is determined by state law, specifically the law of the state of the entity's formation. In iCare's case, the state of Tennessee permits indemnification and exculpation under the following statutory provisions:

  b) AUTHORITY TO INDEMNIFY.

    (1) Except as provided in subsection (d), an LLC may indemnify an individual made a party to a proceeding because such individual is or was a responsible person against liability incurred in the proceeding if the individual:

      (A) Acted in good faith; and

      (B) Reasonably believed:

        (i) In the case of conduct in such individual's official capacity with the LLC that such individual's conduct was in its best interest; and

provide further liability protection for the members who must make business decisions, which from a practical perspective always carry a degree of risk. These provisions would provide further individual protection for members who might negligently breach their duty of care in carrying out their duties for the LLC. But these provisions would not protect them if their actions were deemed to have amounted to gross negligence or arisen out of bad faith conduct.

Once drafted, the Articles of Organization [2] were signed and submitted by the student attorneys to the Secretary of State for review and approval. The Secretary of State's office returned an acknowledgment letter and a date stamped copy of

---

> (ii) In all other cases, that such individual's conduct was at least not opposed to its best interests; and
>
> (C) In the case of any criminal proceeding, had no reasonable cause to believe such individual's conduct was unlawful.

See Tenn. Code Ann. § 48–243–101(b) (2015). [12]

If the LLC is director-managed, a provision eliminating or limiting the personal liability of a director to the LLC or its members for monetary damages for breach of fiduciary duty as a director; provided, that such provision shall not eliminate or limit the liability of a director:

(i) For any breach of the director's duty of loyalty to the LLC or its members;

(ii) For acts or omissions not in good faith, or that involve intentional misconduct or a knowing violation of law; or

(iii) Under § 48–249–307 [13]; and

> (D) A statement to the effect that § 48–249–503(b)(2) [15] shall not apply to the LLC, regardless of whether the LLC falls within the definition of a "family LLC" under § 48–249–102(10). [16]

See Tenn. Code Ann. § 48–249–202 (2015). [17]

the articles of organization [14], indicating that the LLC was officially formed under state law. At this juncture, the student attorneys filed a copy of the articles with the local register of deeds.[11]

2. The Operating Agreement

The student attorneys next asked questions about the operating agreement. An operating agreement is a contract among limited liability company members governing the LLC's business and the members' financial and managerial rights and duties. The operating agreement is analogous to a corporation's bylaws, and controls how the LLC is governed and run. Most states require an LLC to have an operating agreement, in others it is optional.[12] LLCs operating without an operating agreement are governed by the State's default rules contained in the relevant state statute and developed through relevant case law. It is generally preferable to have an operating agreement that either tracks or departs from each of the default state law rules insofar as that tends to mean that the members have at least considered each of those fundamental issues. In other words, there

---

[11]   The register of deeds is an office of the county government in which iCare's offices were located. Under Tennessee law, copies of the articles (already filed with an approval by the Secretary of State) must be filed with the Register of Deeds in the county in which the LLC has its principle office. Articles of amendment, restated articles, and certain other documents must also be filed with the Register of Deeds. Similarly, a copy of a certificate of merger must be filed with the Register of Deeds in the county in which the new or surviving LLC has its principal office. *See* TENN. CODE ANN. § 48–247–103(e) (2012). [18]

[12]   *See* Tenn. Code Ann. § 48–206–101 (2015). [19]

will be no void in the document that will be filled by a state's default rule that has not been considered.

Most small businesses tend to operate as member-managed LLCs—rather than manager-managed or director-managed LLCs. Here, because the founders chose to form a director-managed LLC, the operating agreement needed to include a special section outlining how the directors would be appointed and removed and what authority they would have. In addition, the operating agreement also needed to address other issues such as:

- How would the members' capital contributions (their investments) be made to the LLC and what additional contributions could be made in the future?

- How would the members' percentage interest in the LLC be determined?

- How would the members vote? Based on the amount of capital contributions made? Would decisions be made by simple majority vote or would some decisions require a greater majority vote?

- How would membership interests be transferred in the event of death, disability, or withdrawal?

- How would the interest of the departing member be valued? Could a departing member transfer ownership of their membership interest to outside parties, or will they be required to sell or offer to sell the interest to the remaining members?

- How would profits and losses be allocated to the members? Who would determine if and when distributions will be made?

Once Wyatt and Bell discussed these matters, the student attorneys drafted the Operating Agreement [8] to reflect the agreed upon terms.

3. Additional Matters

The student attorneys next obtained a federal tax Employer Identification Number (EIN) [20] from the Internal Revenue Service and also from the state department of revenue so that the new entity could properly report tax information to the federal and state government. They also instructed the members about how to obtain the necessary business licenses from both the city and county governments.

In addition, they drafted an Action Taken by Written Consent of the Members [21], which amended the Operating Agreement to issue 10% of the financial, membership, and governance interests in iCare Academic LLC to the University of Tennessee Research Foundation. Actions taken by written consent (without a meeting of the members) were specifically allowed by the Operating Agreement in section 9.3. Other actions by taken by written consent of the members included:

- Approval of the initial organizers' actions for the Articles of Organization

- Adoption of the Operating Agreement
- Election of officers
- Approval of previous agreements
- Establishment of a bank account

Because the student attorneys had the benefit of counseling the members in person concerning all aspects of formation of the LLC—including the proper documentation of director actions—there was not a need for a formal initial organizational meeting and a written consent—also known as a "written consent in lieu of a meeting" or just a "consent in lieu"—would suffice. Actions by written consent need to be signed by all of the directors as evidence that they all concur on major decisions concerning the LLC. These actions were then maintained in the LLC Minute Book along with future meeting minutes and Director Resolutions that result from formal board meetings.

III.   RETAINING A CHIEF OPERATING OFFICER

Once iCare Academic LLC was officially formed, Wyatt and Bell next focused on the details of hiring the individual who would run the day-to-day operations of the business. Because of the nature of the position, they originally wanted to structure the relationship using an employment agreement. In addition to clearly describing the job responsibilities of the employee and the commensurate salary, they wanted to address many other aspects of the employment relationship, such as:

- duration of the employment,

- structure and conditions of bonus payments,

- grounds for termination,

- limitations on the employee's ability to compete with the business,

- protection of the business' intellectual property and trade secrets,

- ownership of the employee's work product, and

- dispute resolution provisions.

Wyatt and Bell, in their roles as members and directors, also wanted some control over the employee's ability to terminate his or her employment. While they recognized that they couldn't force someone to continue working for them, they felt that the employee would be more likely to comply with the agreement's terms if there was an incentive to do so or a penalty for not doing so. In this instance, they considered awarding the employee a contingent 2½ % membership interest in the LLC that would vest (i.e., become non-contingent) if the employee stayed for the entirety of the one-year contract. Likewise, they wanted to ensure that the employee met certain performance standards and that the agreement would provide grounds for termination in the event the employee did not meet those standards.

Wyatt and Bell also wanted to ensure that the employee did not mishandle or misappropriate any of the company's intellectual property, trade secrets, or sensitive information. Thus, the student attorneys would include in the agreement a confidentiality and nondisclosure provision to prohibit the employee from disclosing any of iCare's business information or using such information for personal gain. Similarly, a non-compete provision would be included to prevent the employee from competing against the company after employment terminated.[13]

---

[13]   A covenant not to compete in an employment agreement may also be called a "non-compete provision." A covenant not to compete generally requires that, upon leaving the company, an employee agrees not to be employed by their employer's competitors. An employee who signs them either does so as a condition to employment or they may receive compensation for the agreement.

The law regarding enforceability of non-compete provisions varies by jurisdiction and, to some extent, judge to judge. Whether a given judge will enforce a non-compete agreement is difficult to know in advance. Although the interests of employers are important, courts in Tennessee, for example, also give priority to an employee's freedom to choose the type of employment that they desire. As a result, Tennessee courts usually uphold only those covenants that are considered to be reasonable according to the circumstances. Covenants not to compete that a court will categorize as unreasonable include provisions that last for a long duration, that restrict the employee within an unreasonably large geographic area, or that for all practical purposes prevent the employee from earning a living.

Non-compete provisions are also limited by Tennessee law in that they can only apply to competitors who are reasonably related to the industry of the employer. Lastly, the employer needs to have an acceptable business interest which justifies their motives in requiring their employee to sign a covenant not to compete. Tennessee courts look to the following factors to determine if non-compete agreements are enforceable: consideration given for the agreement; danger to the employer if there is no such agreement; economic hardship on the employee created by the covenant; and whether it is against public policy. *See generally* Brian Kingsley

The student attorneys advised the members and directors that an employment agreement is not a one-way street. The contract would bind both iCare and the employee, so it would limit the business's flexibility. This might pose a problem if the members later decided that they did not like the contract terms or that the needs of the business had changed. Under those circumstances, the contract would have to be renegotiated and there would be no guarantee the employee would agree to the desired changes. Unless the employee failed to meet the performance standards outlined in the agreement, any termination by the company without cause would require it to fulfill its obligations under the contract.

The members and directors considered all these issues, as well as the ultimate goal of their venture—which was a successful sale of iCare or its assets. Consequently, they decided they wanted a more simplified arrangement—in the nature of consultant and independent contractor rather than employer and employee.

Early on in the process Wyatt and Bell had been working with Henry King, an M.B.A. student at the Haslam College of Business at the University of Tennessee. The members chose to continue working

---

Krumm, *Covenants Not to Compete: Time for Legislation and Judicial Reform in Tennessee*, 35 U. MEM. L. REV. 447 (2005).

In contrast, covenants not to compete are largely unenforceable in California unless entered into as part of the sale of someone's business. This illustrates why an attorney must know or research applicable law governing various contract provisions in each affected jurisdiction. Retaining local counsel in foreign jurisdictions is often required and always a good idea.

with King and he and iCare entered into a Consulting Agreement [22]. Under this agreement, iCare Academic retained King as a consultant and independent contractor, and King agreed to "serve the Company as a consultant regarding Mergers, Acquisitions, and Asset Sales." In exchange, iCare Academic agreed to pay King a "consulting fee" of $115,000 per year "payable within 90 days of the successful sale of the company or certain company assets to a purchasing party." The Consulting Agreement contained a confidentiality and non-disclosure provision that applied during and after the consulting period, as well as a non-compete provision that applied during the consulting period.

QUESTIONS

1.   What type of business entity did the founders decide on for iCare?

2.   What are some of the advantages of this form of entity?

3.   What was the UT College of Law Business Law Clinic originally consulted for?

4.   How and why did this engagement expand?

5.   What are articles of organization and what must they generally contain?

6.   What additional provisions were included in iCare Academic LLC's articles of organization?

7.   What other document related to LLCs that is required in most states, and what does it do?

8.   What did iCare Academic operating agreement address?

9. Under iCare Academic's operating agreement how were financial and governance rights allocated among the members?

10. Did this allocation change? If yes, how?

11. What was an important provision Wyatt and Bell wanted in Consulting Agreement?

12. Why was this provision important to them?

CHAPTER 2

OBTAINING INITIAL
BUSINESS FINANCING

I. OBTAINING INITIAL
SHORT-TERM FINANCING

Once Harry King, the new consultant and Chief Operating Officer, was brought on board, he was given the responsibility of crafting the core business strategy. This primarily involved identifying and quantifying the market potential for iCare and developing a sound business plan that would chart the course to transform this good idea into a sustainable business. Preliminary analysis projected the potential market for iCare to be $46 million in sales. Based on the initial research for the business plan and discussion with trusted business advisors, additional testing with other schools would be required to further refine the software so that it would address the needs of a broader market of potential users. To accomplish this task, and to acquire additional programming support, there was a need for both short-term and long-term financing.

Because iCare did not have any tangible assets[1] that could be used as collateral, banks were unwilling to loan money to iCare without getting a personal guarantee from the directors of the company. As a result, three of the members, Wyatt, Bell, and Indranoi agreed to loan money from their personal

---

[1]   The intellectual property created by the founders—the iCare system—was an intangible, intellectual property asset.

finances for immediate operating capital, until longer term financing could be obtained. Clinic student attorneys prepared the appropriate documents to memorialize the transaction. The loan was evidenced by a Promissory Note and Loan Agreement [23] between each individual lending the money and iCare. A promissory note is a document that constitutes a written, signed, unconditional promise to pay an amount of money on certain terms, like over a set period of time, with interest, with fees, and similar charges. In this case, each of the three members loaned iCare $10,000 and iCare issued its promissory note in the principal amount of $10,000 payable in 24 monthly installments at 14% interest, compounded monthly.

In addition, each individual lender and iCare entered into a security agreement [24] which gave the lender a security interest in the assets of iCare. A security agreement is an agreement a borrower signs that gives a lender a present, non-possessory property interest in particular assets called a "security interest" or a "lien." Basically, the security agreement provides that if the borrower fails to make payments under the promissory note, the lender can declare the borrower to be in default and can cause the assets subject to the lien to be sold, with the proceeds applied to satisfy the obligations due under the promissory note. In other words, upon the borrower's default, the lender can foreclose on the collateral.

In this case, iCare was willing to give the lending members a security interest in all of its tangible and intangible assets, including both those it currently owned and those it would later acquire, which are referred to as "after-acquired property." In the event that the business failed or did not repay the promissory note for other reasons, each of the members would be able to cause those assets to be sold. The student attorneys then filed a UCC-1 Financing Statement [25] with the Secretary of State as public notice of the loan and to establish priority in the collateral.

By filing a UCC-1 form and thus giving the whole world constructive notice of the lien, the three lenders were preventing a later lender or someone else that obtained a lien—like a judgment lien if iCare were sued and found liable—from having a superior claim to the assets. When collateral is foreclosed upon and sold, the proceeds are applied and distributed to secured creditors in order of priority—the loan secured by the 1st lien gets paid first, then the loan secured by the 2nd lien, and so on until the proceeds are exhausted (any proceeds remaining after paying secured creditors are paid to the borrower, but this rarely happens). The UCC-1 provides legal notice "to the world" of the lender's lien, making it "fair" that it receive priority over later claims. Filing the UCC-1 with the secretary of state is the "magic step" that locks in a lender's priority if it is done correctly.

II. ASSESSING LONG-TERM FINANCING OPTIONS

Business financing generally comes in the form of (1) debt financing—money obtained through loans that must be repaid over time; (2) equity financing—money obtained in exchange for an ownership or "equity" interest in the business; or (3) a hybrid involving debt than can be converted into equity. In some cases, Small Business Innovation Research Grants can be obtained through the National Science Foundation.

Debt financing takes the form of loans that must be repaid over time with interest. Businesses can borrow money over the short term (less than one year) or long term (more than one year). The main sources of debt financing are banks and government agencies, such as the Small Business Association (the "SBA"). Debt financing offers businesses a tax advantage, because the interest paid on loans is generally tax deductible. However, new businesses sometimes find it difficult to make regular loan payments because they have irregular cash flow. Carrying too much debt can also increase the perceived risk associated with the business, making it unattractive to investors and thus reducing the company's ability to raise additional capital in the future.

The directors decided against pursuing a General Small Business Loan under the SBA loan guarantee program. While the opportunity to secure a SBA loan looked promising, it featured some negatives as well. The SBA program is a loan guarantee program that works with local lenders to establish or expand a new business. Because the loan is guaranteed by the federal government, banks are more likely to lend to a small business that does not have operating income or significant assets that can be used for collateral. However, an SBA loan would require the members (those individuals holding 20 percent or more equity in the company) to sign personal guarantees, making them personally liable if iCare did not repay the loan. The members wanted to maintain the separateness of their obligations from those of the company, so the SBA loan option was eliminated.

Equity financing takes the form of money obtained from investors in exchange for an ownership share in the business. The investors become shareholders or members in the company. This ownership can take the form of either common or preferred stock, or similar forms of LLC membership interest. Preferred shares can be structured so that the investor can convert the preferred shares into common stock (in which case they are known as convertible preferred stock) at some time in the future at an advantageous rate in the event that the company is purchased or goes public. Preferred stock may also offer the investor a level of protection by providing priority over the common shareholder in the liquidation of the assets of the company in the event that it fails. Also, priority is typically given to preferred shares for any dividend that might be issued from profits of the corporation. In other words, in the event that the corporation pays out any dividends, the preferred shareholders would receive payment before common shareholders. While preferred shareholders do not have the same voting rights as common shareholders, these shares can include voting provisions on special matters like raising corporate debt, thus protecting the investment of the preferred shareholders.

Generally, sources of equity financing are either Angel Investors[2] or Venture Capitalists.[3] Often,

---

[2]   An angel investor is an affluent individual who provides capital for a business start-up, usually in exchange for debt that is convertible into equity or just ownership equity. Angel investors are often retired entrepreneurs or executives who may be interested in angel investing for reasons that go beyond pure monetary return. These include wanting to keep abreast of current developments in a particular business arena, mentoring another generation of entrepreneurs, and making use of their experience and networks on a less than full-time basis. Thus, in addition to funds, angel investors can often provide valuable management advice and important contacts. Because there are no public exchanges listing their securities, private companies meet angel investors in several ways, including referrals from the investors' trusted sources and other business contacts; at investor conferences and symposia; and at meetings organized by groups of "angels" where companies pitch directly to investors generally in face-to-face meetings. There is no set investment amount for angel investors and the range can go anywhere from a few thousand to a few million dollars. Because a large percentage of angel investments are lost completely when early-stage companies fail, professional angel investors seek investments that have the potential to return at least 10 or more times their original investment within five years through a well-defined exit strategy such as an initial public offering or acquisition by another company.

[3]   Venture capital (or "VC") is financial capital provided to early-stage, high-potential, high risk, growth startup companies. The venture capital fund makes money by owning equity in the companies it invests in, which usually have a novel technology or business model in high technology industries. Generally, venture capitalists can be viewed as financial intermediaries, meaning they first must convince wealthy individuals, pension funds, corporations, and foundations to trust the venture capitalists with their money, which the venture capitalists will use to make equity

angel and venture capital investors will also request
to be appointed to the board of directors so they can
closely monitor and participate in the direction of the
corporation and/or require that a Chief Executive
Officer (CEO) of their choosing be installed to run the
day to day operations of the corporation. The iCare
directors were reluctant to pursue financing through
the use of either Angel Investors or Venture
Capitalists. Both financing sources would require the
directors to relinquish a significant portion of their
ownership interest through either the use of debt
convertible into an equity interest in the company or
an outright equity investment in the company.

A hybrid of debt financing and equity financing is
obtaining money in exchange for convertible debt—
either a convertible bond or note. Convertible debt
allows the holder to convert it into a specified number
of shares of common stock in the issuing company or

---

investments in privately held companies. Venture capitalists also
are expected to nurture the companies in which they invest by
providing advice and contacts, in order to increase the likelihood
of reaching an initial public offering or sale when the company's
valuation increases. The need for high returns makes venture
funding an expensive capital source for companies and most
suitable for businesses having large up-front capital requirements
that cannot be financed by cheaper alternatives (such as debt).
That is most commonly the case for businesses involving
development of intellectual property whose value is unproven. In
turn, this explains why venture capital is most prevalent in the
fast-growing technology and life sciences (or biotechnology) fields.
If a company has the qualities venture capitalists seek—including
a solid business plan, a good management team, investment, and
passion from the founders, a good potential to exit the investment
before the end of their funding cycle, and target minimum returns
in excess of forty percent per year—it will find it easier to raise
venture capital.

cash of equal value. It is a hybrid security with debt- and equity-like features. Convertible debt is much like preferred stock, but sits one rung up on the priority ladder above preferred stock, meaning that in the event of bankruptcy or liquidation, the holder of convertible debt will be paid before the holders of preferred stock. Convertible debt is most often issued by companies with a low credit rating and high growth potential. To compensate for having additional value through the option to convert the debt to stock, convertible debt typically has an interest rate lower than that of similar, non-convertible debt. The investor receives the potential upside of conversion into equity while protecting itself from downside risk with cash flow from the interest payments and the return of principal upon maturity before conversion. The debt instrument may also receive priority over equity investors in the event of liquidation. Although company debt would not subject the directors to any personal responsibility to repay the investment in the event that the company failed, they did not want to risk losing the upside potential of sharing the potential profits and potentially losing management control over the direction of the company. This ruled out the use of convertible debt.

III. OBTAINING A SMALL BUSINESS INNOVATION RESEARCH GRANT

The National Science Foundation's SBIR grant program is designed to encourage domestic small businesses to engage in Federal Research/Research and Development that has the potential for commercialization.[4] If iCare's proposal was approved, the SBIR Grant would provide iCare with Phase I funding of up to $150,000 over a period of 24 months. With such funding, iCare could pursue beta-testing[5] of the system with other universities, further refine the software to meet the needs of a broader constituency, and obtain the programming support activities necessary to perfect the system. If necessary, iCare might also be eligible for additional financing without the need to repay the federal government for the grants.[6] The directors decided to

---

[4]   The primary purpose of federal research is to discover and advance fundamental scientific and technical knowledge whereas research and development attempts to take that fundamental research and develop valuable new products, processes and services. The purpose of the SBIR program is to provide incentives to increase private- sector commercialization of innovations derived from federally funded basic research which promote practical applications for the technology which has the added benefit of stimulating economic activity.

[5]   Beta-testing is a test for a computer software product prior to commercial release. Beta-testing is the last stage of testing and normally can involve sending the product to beta-test sites outside the company for real-world exposure or offering the product for a free trial download, typically with an agreement to provide feedback, user data and suggested improvements.

[6]   The mission of the SBIR program is to support scientific excellence and technological innovation through the investment of federal research funds in critical American priorities to build a strong national economy. The program's goals are to stimulate technological innovation, foster and encourage participation in innovation and entrepreneurship by socially and economically disadvantaged persons, and increase private-sector commercialization of innovations derived from federal research and development funding. SBIR funding provides grants in three phases:

Phase I. The objective of Phase I is to establish the technical merit, feasibility, and commercial potential of the proposed Federal Research /R&D efforts and to determine the quality

pursue this "free money" option and avoid having iCare (or themselves) incur additional debt or divest themselves of a significant portion of the equity in the company.

Funding under the SBIR program was not a certainty, however. The program is a highly competitive one that required the iCare team to prepare a detailed proposal. SBIR submission guidelines set forth these requirements:

- Project Summary—an overview of the intellectual merit and societal impact that would result from the commercialization of iCare;

---

of performance of the small business awardee organization prior to providing further federal support in Phase II. SBIR Phase I awards normally do not exceed $150,000 and have a six-month period of performance.

Phase II. The objective of Phase II is to continue the Federal Research/R&D efforts initiated in Phase I. Funding is based on the results achieved in Phase I and the scientific and technical merit and commercial potential of the project proposed in Phase II. Generally, only Phase I awardees are eligible for a Phase II award. SBIR Phase II awards normally do not exceed $1,000,000 and have a two-year period of performance.

Phase III. The objective of Phase III, where appropriate, is for the small business to pursue commercialization objectives resulting from the Phase I and Phase II Federal Research/R&D activities. The SBIR program does not fund Phase III awards. In some federal agencies, Phase III may involve follow-on non-SBIR funded R&D or production contracts for products, processes, or services intended for use by the federal government.

U.S. SMALL BUS. ADMIN., *About SBIR* [92], SBIR/STTR

- Project Description—a detailed description of the significance of the invention in the marketplace as well as an outline of the research plan and methodology to be used, along with the technical expertise and experience of the individuals participating in the project;

- Budget Justification—a breakdown of the personnel, equipment, travel, and overhead and indirect costs associated with the research;

- Facilities, Equipment, and Other Resources— an explanation of contributions that will be made from other strategic partners both inside and outside of the university.

Because iCare did not yet have a formal business plan, the preparation of the grant proposal would serve to force the team to: (1) create a set of business goals; (2) provide the reasons why these goals were attainable; and (3) describe the steps for reaching those goals; all with supporting financial data and clearly articulated assumptions. The grant proposal would also contain background information about the organization and the team attempting to reach those goals.

After the team completed the process, the iCare SBIR grant proposal [26] covered the critical aspects of the business planning process and clearly articulated iCare's vision and strategy, along with operating plans covering market assessment as well as financial and human resource requirements. The substance of the proposal, like a business plan, outlined the fundamental assumptions and the extrapolations from those assumptions that predict that the business can be successful.

The iCare SBIR proposal [26] was submitted to the National Science Foundation on December 30, 2009 by Dr. Xueping Li, who was listed as the Principal Investigator (the "PI")[7] on the project. The grant proposal was a success. Based upon the information provided in the proposal, the iCare team received a Phase I grant in the amount of $150,000, with a projected start date of July 1, 2010.[8] With this funding, iCare could take the next steps toward beta-testing and further refining the system before taking it to market.

QUESTIONS

1. What was the source of iCare's initial financing?

2. How were these loans documented?

3. What were terms of the loan transactions?

---

[7] The principal investigator is the individual with the primary responsibility for the primary scientific and technical direction of the project. The PI is not required to have US citizenship, but the PI must legally reside in the United States and must be available to perform the research proposed for the duration of the project. The individual who is the PI must be from the small business and meet the primary employment requirement that more than one half of the PI's time is spent in the employ of the small business at the time of award and during the conduct of the proposed project.

[8] *See*, Award Abstract #1013586 [27], SBIR Phase I: Usability of iCare: An Academic Electronic Health Record Clinical Simulation Tool.

4. What are the most common forms of business financing?

5. Please briefly explain each of these forms of financing.

6. Did iCare pursue any of these more common forms of business financing? Why or Why not?

7. Why do you think iCare's SBIR Grant Proposal [26] was successful? Review the proposal as well as the mission of the SBIR Grant program to answer this question.

CHAPTER 3

BUSINESS ASSETS: INTELLECTUAL PROPERTY PROTECTION, LICENSING, AND BETA-TESTING

I. THE NATURE OF INTELLECTUAL PROPERTY

Intellectual property consists of property rights in innovations and distinguishing marks.[1] In the United States, innovations are primarily protected by federal copyright and patent law and state trade secret law.[2]

A. COPYRIGHT PROTECTION

The Copyright Act protects "original works of authorship fixed in any tangible medium of expression, now known or later developed, from which they can be perceived, reproduced, or otherwise communicated, either directly or with the aid of a machine or device." 17 U.S.C. § 102(a) [29]. Under § 102(a), works of authorship include:

- literary works;

- musical works, including any accompanying words;

---

[1] George W. Kuney & Donna C. Looper, MASTERING INTELLECTUAL PROPERTY (Carolina Academic Press 2009).

[2] In addition, federal and state trademark law allows providers of goods and services to distinguish their products from those of their competitors. The goodwill associated with the trademark can be among a business's most important assets.

- dramatic works, including any accompanying music;

- pantomimes and choreographic works;

- pictorial, graphic, and sculptural works;

- motion pictures and other audiovisual works;

- sound recordings; and

- architectural works.

The types of copyrightable works expand as technology advances. For example, the copyrightability of computer programs was uncertain in the last quarter of the twentieth century. Because computer programs cannot be expressed without the aid of a computer, there were doubts as to whether the programs were copyrightable. Congress concluded that computer programs should be eligible for protection and amended the Copyright Act to specifically include computer programs in 1980. See 17 U.S.C. §§ 101 & 117 (defining a computer program as "set of statements or instructions to be used directly or indirectly in a computer in order to bring about a certain result"). The literal elements of the computer software (the source code) are copyrightable as a tangible medium of expression. In this way, computer programs are protected as literary works.[3] The non-literal elements of the computer program, "the structure, sequence and organization of the program, the user interface, and the function, or purpose, of the

---

[3]　　Apple Computer, Inc. v. Franklin Computer Corp., 714 F.2d 1240 (3d Cir. 1983).

program,"[4] are also copyrightable as long as they are not the only possible expression of an underlying idea. This is because copyright law protects the form of expression rather than the subject matter itself.

Copyright protection gives the author the exclusive right to make copies, determine how they can be distributed (e.g., online vs. print, free or with a fee), make changes to the original copyrighted work, and to perform or display the work publicly. Copyright protection begins "at creation"—when the work is fixed in a tangible form, 17 U.S.C. § 101, and lasts for the life of the author or creator plus 70 years. 17 U.S.C. § 302(a). Even though a work is copyrighted at the moment of creation, the author must also include a notice to others on copies of the work, e.g. "© 2016 University of Tennessee. All rights reserved." See 17 U.S.C. §§ 401, 402. Omission of a copyright notice will generally invalidate the copyright in a work, unless notice has been omitted from a relatively small number of copies, or registration of the work is made before or within five years from the time of publication and reasonable efforts are made to add copyright notices to all copies after the omission has been discovered. 17 U.S.C. §§ 405.

To more formally protect a work, there is a registration process for copyrights through the *Copyright Office of the Library of Congress* [30]. The benefits of registration are substantial. Authors must have registered their copyright in order to commence

---

⁴   Johnson Controls, Inc. v. Phoenix Control Systems, Inc., 886 F.2d 1173 (9th Cir. 1989).

legal action for copyright infringement. Furthermore, if a work is infringed upon before it is registered, the holder of the copyright will not be able to seek statutory damages or attorneys' fees from the infringing party unless registration is secured within three months of the work's first publication. Registration made within five years after the work's first publication constitutes prima facie evidence of the validity of the copyright. 17 U.S.C. §§ 408, 410.

Accordingly, copyright protection for the computer program for the iCare Academic EHR clinical simulation tool began when it was fixed in tangible medium by Xueping Li and Chayawat Indranoi in early 2009. iCare Academic LLC would also register their copyrights [82] in this innovation.

B. PATENT PROTECTION

A patent—short for "letters patent"—is the government's grant to its holder of a limited monopoly that enables the holder to exclude others from making, using, selling, importing, or offering the patented invention for sale for a fixed period of time—generally 20 years from when the patent application was filed. 35 U.S.C. § 154(a)(2). In return for this grant of temporary exclusivity, patent applicants must reveal information that would allow the invention to be reproduced.

The Patent Act allows inventors to obtain patents on "any new and useful process, machine, manufacture, or composition of matter, or any new and useful improvement thereof." 35 U.S.C. § 101. Additionally, an invention must be non-obvious in order to qualify for a patent. The key requirements for patentability are: (1) novelty (§§ 101–102), (2) utility (§ 101), and (3) non-obviousness (§ 103).

- For an invention to be new or "novel" under § 102, it must, at the time of filing, differ from previously known inventions and pre-existing knowledge in the field ("prior art").

- To be "useful" under § 101, an invention need only be minimally operable towards some practical purpose.

- To be "non-obvious" under § 103, the invention must be different enough from the prior art that it would not be obvious to "a person having ordinary skill in the art."

"Laws of nature, natural phenomena, and abstract ideas are not patentable," however.[5] Hence, for a computer program or software to be eligible for patent protection, the program or software must do more than merely use computer technology to implement an abstract idea. For example in *Alice Corp. Pty. Ltd. v. CLS Bank Intern.*, 134 S.Ct. 2347, 2352 (2014), patents had been issued for a "computer-implemented scheme for mitigating 'settlement risk' (*i.e.,* the risk that only one party to a financial transaction will pay what it owes) by using a third-party intermediary." The Supreme Court, however, held that the computer scheme was ineligible for patent protection because: "The claims at issue are drawn to the abstract idea of intermediated

---

[5]   Association for Molecular Pathology v. Myriad Genetics, Inc., 133 S. Ct. 2107, 2116 (2013). [83]

settlement, and that merely requiring generic computer implementation fails to transform that abstract idea into a patent-eligible invention." Thus a computer program or software must add significantly more than "generic computing." The invention should involve a particular, technological way of doing something with a computer.

A patent was not sought for the iCare technology.

C. TRADE SECRET PROTECTION

In some instances, maintaining the innovation as a trade secret may be the form of protection. Trade secrets allow businesses to protect proprietary information and ideas that do not qualify for protection as a patent or copyright. Moreover, a business may choose trade secret protection instead of patent and copyright protection to avoid the limitations of patent and copyright laws. For example, a patent applicant must enter the content of its application into the public record in order to obtain a patent, but there is no such requirement to protect an innovation as a trade secret. Furthermore, common law trade secret protection may be broader than the finite terms of patent and copyright protections. Trade secrets remain protected indefinitely as long as their holder takes the necessary steps to keep them secret, but once the information is no longer secret, trade secret protection is no longer available. Thus, precautions against the disclosure of trade secrets are very important.

In contrast to patents and copyrights, which are governed by federal law, trade secrets are derived from state law.[6] A trade secret involves information that: (1) is not a matter of general knowledge and is not readily ascertainable; (2) is commercially valuable or gives the proprietor an economic advantage because of its secrecy; and (3) is guarded by reasonable means to maintain its secrecy. Technical information—including aspects of computer programs or software, business information, and even know-how may be protectable as trade secrets. In iCare's case the goal was to widely distribute the EHR clinical simulation tool, although information regarding the program was kept confidential through beta testing and in the pre-sale stages.

II. THE UNIQUE NATURE OF INTELLECTUAL PROPERTY OWNERSHIP IN THE UNIVERSITY SETTING

Generally speaking, ownership of an innovation is based on the context within which it was created. If an innovation is created by an employee acting in the scope of employment in a private business, the employee is viewed to be producing the innovation for or on behalf of that business—this is called the "work for hire" or "work made for hire" doctrine. See, e.g., 17 U.S.C. § 101 of the Copyright Act (defining work made for hire). Thus, innovations created within the

---

6   Much of the state law is based upon or reflected in the Restatement (First) of Torts § 757, the Uniform Trade Secrets Act, and the Restatement (Third) of Unfair Competition § 39.

scope of employment are the property of the employer, not the employee. In most instances, written employment agreements will stipulate that anything produced for work purposes will remain the property of the business.[7]

Like most employers, the University of Tennessee is the original owner of any intellectual property developed by university employees during the course of employment, or developed by anyone using university facilities, funds, or equipment.[8] This policy [28] includes students, faculty, and outside contributors. As a general rule, the researcher will have assigned the innovation to the university well in advance of the time that the innovation is actually reduced to practice (that is, built or assembled in usable form). It is common for the assignment to

---

[7] Pre-Innovation Assignments are included in many employment agreements and serve to give the employer rights to all inventions of the employee. Under a pre-innovation assignment, the employee must turn over all ownership rights over anything invented or created while the employee works for the employer. The pre-innovation assignment occurs at the outset of employment before anything is actually invented or created by the employee during the course of employment.

[8] Typically, faculty and students that author traditional academic works (e.g., scholarly publications, curriculum development, books, teaching materials, theses, and course notes) are the owners of that intellectual property. However, if the university is the initiator of that work (e.g., creation of a new online course), it may or may not be considered traditional academic work. Ownership will depend on circumstances surrounding its development and the extent of university resources used. It should be noted that invention ownership and copyright ownership may be different. As an example, author(s) of a paper describing an invention may own the copyright for that paper, but the university may own the invention described in the paper.

constitute part of the university researcher's employment agreement. However, in the case of patents, if an invention was created at the university as a result of federal funding, federal law imposes an additional set of requirements with which the university and the inventor must comply.[9]

III. INTELLECTUAL PROPERTY PROTECTION, EVALUATION, AND MANAGEMENT

Within this broad university policy[10] and federal statutory framework, the University of Tennessee's Office of Technology Transfer ("UTRF") is charged with protecting the intellectual property created on campus, evaluating its commercial value in the marketplace, and managing the technology transfer process. Employees of UTRF are the first members of the university community outside of the researcher's department to receive official notice that the researcher has an invention that may merit protection. UT's Policy divides intellectual property into two categories, Inventions and Creations. Inventions are defined as "All inventions, discoveries, computer programs, software and/or codes, methods, uses, products or combinations, whether or not patented or patentable at any time under the Federal Patent Act as now existing or hereafter amended or supplemented." Creations are defined as "Written

---

9 See the Bayh-Dole Act; also known as the University and Small Business Patent Procedures Act of 1980, 35 U.S.C. §§ 200–212.

10 See The University of Tennessee Policies. [28]

creations, recorded creations, arts and crafts, and mediated." The notice is in the form of an invention or creation disclosure. A typical invention disclosure contains information such as:

- the title of the invention;

- an abstract (approximately 250 words) describing the invention;

- names of co-inventors divided into two categories based on whether they are employed by the university or not;

- dates that the invention was conceived of and reduced to practice, including the existence of documentation verifying those dates (usually in the form of laboratory notebooks containing experimental design and results);

- funding sources that provided monetary support for the research that produced the invention, including private sources and federal, state, and municipal agencies;

- names of any companies or particular industries that the inventor believes may have an interest in licensing the invention; and

- a distribution schedule assigning the percentage of royalties that each co-inventor should receive of any proceeds that may eventually be allocated to the inventors; and

- signatures of all inventors and co-inventors.

Once UTRF receives an invention disclosure, a licensing associate is assigned to assess if the invention is patentable and if so, how much time they have to file a patent based upon the requirements of the statutory bar or filing deadline. If the subject invention is believed to be patentable, the licensing agent must then assess whether the invention is marketable. The mere fact that an invention is novel and may be useful does not guarantee that anyone will be interested in paying money to license it, and it certainly does not guarantee that there will be enough interest in licensing the invention for UTRF to recoup the money that it would have to spend to patent the invention and bring it to market. The licensing associate will meet with the researcher to discuss the invention and ask several questions to assess both the current status and future potential of the idea. This may include engaging outside patent attorneys, consultants, and industry experts to validate the idea and the market need. Potential licensees are also investigated in this process— inventors are critical contributors in this phase as they often have industry contacts that may be interested in their work.

During this process, the technology also will be evaluated for its best commercialization path. A technology that is an improvement to a technology that already exists or is a new technology but only has one application is typically licensed to an existing company that already has the resources in place in that particular market area. If the technology is a "platform" technology, meaning that it has a multitude of applications in a wide variety of market areas, it often is a candidate for a start-up company. Because start-up company investors want to maximize their potential profits and minimize the risk of their investment, they look for an invention that has a wide variety of potential market applications. This is typically a more difficult path to commercialization, but can be much more lucrative if done properly.

During this evaluation process, the licensing agent will also consider whether the invention should more appropriately be considered for copyright or trade secret protection.

After UTRF's preliminary assessment is complete, the licensing associate and business professionals convene to conduct a review of the technology—called the "triage" process. After consulting with people with different backgrounds and industry expertise, this triage team will make a preliminary decision on whether or not the technology will be pursued. Once this decision has been made, the licensing associate will contact the inventor to discuss the decision. Occasionally during this discussion, new information may be obtained that may change the outcome, requiring a reconvening of the triage team for another review and decision.

If the technology appears protectable and market-viable, UTRF will reach out to potential companies or entrepreneurs to test the market response and identify those that may be interested in licensing the technology. During the marketing campaign, the hopeful outcome is that a company becomes interested in learning more about the invention so that they can determine whether they want to license it. During this pre-licensing stage, representatives from a prospective company are asked to sign a Non-Disclosure Agreement (NDA). This document is used by UTRF to protect information that has not been publicly disclosed about the invention from being misappropriated by the reviewing company. The representatives may also be asked to sign a Material Transfer Agreement (MTA) if the company wants to evaluate any materials that have been developed by the researcher. During this evaluation process, a company may enter into an Option Agreement in order to place a hold on the technology while it does additional technical or business evaluation on the technology. In this case, UTRF will grant the company a short-term right (typically for six months) to finish its evaluations. The company will usually pay a small fixed fee to UTRF in exchange for taking the technology off the market.

IV. OBTAINING A LICENSE FOR USE OF THE INTELLECTUAL PROPERTY

After evaluating the invention disclosure submitted by Wyatt and Bell, and recognizing their desire to bring their invention to market themselves, the triage team recommended that UTRF license the technology back to iCare. The triage team reasoned that the inventors were in the best position to perform the necessary testing and refinement of the EHR system in order to effectively bring it to market. As academics in the health care field, they understood the market for the product probably as well as or better than anyone else. Furthermore, they had a passion for their invention. Since they originally developed it for their own use, they were intimately aware of the benefits that it could bring to the education of other health care professionals.

Before Wyatt and Bell could enter into a license agreement where the rights to the technology were officially transferred to iCare, a Basic Agreement [31] would have to be completed. A Basic Agreement officially assigns the rights in the technology from the university to UTRF, and it sets out the financial relationship among the inventors (e.g., should revenues be obtained, how the royalties will be split between the inventors and the university). This agreement is initiated by UTRF, and involves discussions with all of the inventors on any particular technology. In this case, the Basic Agreement established a 50% split between the university and the four inventors of the iCare technology, with each of the inventors receiving 25% of the 50% (or 1/8) share of any potential income generated from the technology.

Once the Basic Agreement was completed, Wyatt and Bell met with clinic student attorneys to discuss the factors that should be considered when negotiating the Intellectual Property License Agreement with UTRF. The student attorneys explained that the process would start with the drafting of a term sheet which would set forth the business terms of the license agreement. A term sheet is typically a bullet-point document outlining the material terms and conditions of a business agreement. After a term sheet has been prepared, it is used to guide legal counsel in the preparation of a proposed final agreement. A term sheet implies the conditions of a business transaction, as proposed by a party. It may be either binding or non-binding. Term sheets are very similar to letters of intent ("LOI") in that they are both preliminary, mostly non-binding documents meant to record two or more parties' intentions to attempt to enter into a future agreement based on specified (but incomplete or preliminary) terms. The difference between the two is slight and mostly a matter of style: an LOI is typically written in letter form and focuses on the parties' intentions, while a term sheet skips most of the formalities and usually just lists deal terms in bullet-point or similar format. With both LOI and term sheets, the drafter should make clear that they are merely preliminary and not the binding agreement, unless the intent is otherwise.

There are many factors to consider when developing a term sheet, including the type of technology involved, the significance of the technology in the market, the extent of development needed to get the technology ready for market introduction, and the financial resources available to develop the company. Typical terms to be considered when negotiating a licensing agreement include:

- *Exclusivity*—Most start-ups need an exclusive license to the intellectual property (IP), which means that no other company will be able to license the technology from UTRF. This provides a competitive advantage to the company, but is riskier for UTRF. This is because the university is relying solely on a brand new, inexperienced company to successfully commercialize the technology.

- *Field of Use*—Field of use refers to a defined area of permissible operation, such as in a particular industry segment. Most start-ups need multiple fields of use to attract significant investment capital. But the broader the scope, the riskier it becomes for UTRF.

- *Territory*—Licenses can be granted for use worldwide or in more narrowly defined geographical areas. Start-ups typically want worldwide use.

- *License or Option Fee*—A license fee may be used for several reasons, including covering sunk costs, extracting a premium for the technology demand, or to ensure that a buyer is serious about commercializing the IP. UTRF typically keeps this fee to a minimum or exchanges it for equity in the company to reduce the cash burden on a start-up company.

- *Royalty Rates*—These are fees paid to UTRF for the right to sell products and/or services based on the licensed IP. Royalties are typically a percentage of net revenues from sales or a fixed price per unit sold. The amount depends on a number of factors, including the industry, the value of the IP relative to the total value of the final product, the maturity of the IP (how close it is to being fully developed), and the growth of the market.

- *Minimum Royalties*—Most license agreements will ask for a minimum fixed payment of royalties after development is complete, regardless of the amount of sales of the product. This is to ensure that the company continues to work toward commercializing the product (so that a technology isn't licensed and then "parked" on a shelf). If the minimum amount is below what calculated royalties should be, UTRF credits it towards the entire royalty payment. For example, let's say that a license agreement has a royalty rate of 5% of net sales and minimum royalties of $3,000 per year, starting in year 3 of the license agreement. If the company has $50,000 in net sales in year 3, the calculated royalty rate payable at the end of the year to UTRF is $2,500 (5% × $50,000). Because the minimum royalties are $3,000, the company would have to pay UTRF an additional $500 in royalties. On the other hand, if net sales are $200,000, the company would owe UTRF $10,000 in royalties (5% × $100,000). That exceeds the minimum royalty amount of $3,000 so the company pays only the $10,000 in royalties.

- *Equity*—Sometimes UTRF will accept an ownership stake in the company in lieu of other compensation (license fees and/or reduced royalty rates). The decision and the amount of equity will depend on many factors, including UTRF's assessment of the potential success of the company, the amount of money that UTRF has invested in the technology, potential investors, and discussions with the inventor.

- *Sublicense Revenues*—Typically start-ups will receive the rights to sublicense the technology to other companies (often for other application development or distribution rights). In addition to any standard royalty rates, UTRF will also take a percentage of any additional fees that the start-up company receives from the sublicense.

- *Patent Reimbursement*—Except in rare cases, UTRF always requires reimbursement of patent costs (so that patent funds are available for future technologies).

- *Patent Prosecution and Infringement*—Once the technology is licensed, all future patent expenses will be borne by the start-up. The start-up also takes responsibility for defending a patent in court if infringement is alleged.

- *Performance Milestones*—To ensure that the technology is commercialized in a timely manner, UTRF and the start-up jointly agree on performance milestones. These milestones typically include dates for business plan completion, prototype development, and timing for first revenues. If milestones are not met, UTRF will determine whether to modify or terminate the license agreement.

- *Reserved Rights*—In all license agreements, UTRF will reserve the right to use the technology for research purposes. If federal funding has been involved in its development, the federal government may have "march-in rights," which means that they can issue a new license to another party for the technology if the start-up company fails to make the product available to the public on reasonable terms.

- *Indemnification*—The start-up company will take on all of the technical and market risk for the technology. By state law, the university cannot be held liable if the technology does not work or the market does not adopt the product.

The student attorneys informed Wyatt and Bell that the reserved rights and indemnification terms were nonnegotiable due to considerations of federal and state law, as well as university policy. The rest of the terms however could be negotiated, but were in essence business decisions that required the consensus of all the iCare members. The members agreed that they would like an exclusive worldwide license for all potential markets that their EHR system could effectively enter. In addition, since operating capital was scarce, they were willing to give UTRF an equity stake in iCare instead of minimum royalties.[11]

Wyatt and Bell then met with UTRF management to discuss the term sheet that would lead to the drafting of a licensing agreement between the parties. Because UTRF did not have to provide initial funding to patent the subject technology, its investment was limited to time spent evaluating the invention for purposes of commercialization. As such, UTRF was willing to agree to forgo payments of minimum royalties in exchange for a 10 percent equity stake in iCare. In turn, because UTRF would be participating as an equity member in iCare and have input into the strategic management of the venture, UTRF was also willing to grant the entity an exclusive worldwide license for any potential market in which the technology could be used.

The discussions concerning the performance milestones were the most time consuming. Wyatt and Bell relied primarily on the schedule that was developed for the SBIR proposal which outlined a July 1, 2010 start date and a July 1, 2012 finish date. During this time, student focus groups would be conducted, beta-testing by other university nursing programs would be concluded and the resulting changes to the programming of the software package would be completed. Satisfied with these milestones, UTRF entered into a software licensing agreement [32] with iCare.

---

[11]   Funds that were available from the SBIR grant could not be used for purposes of paying minimum royalties.

V. BETA-TESTING AND BETA-TESTING SUBLICENSE AGREEMENTS

Beta-testing is the last important step that software developers undertake before they launch new software. Software systems at their beta stages are not fully developed and perhaps not completely functional. The purpose of beta-testing is to give the developers a first look and a brief glimpse of what it can do for the users before its final launching in the market. Having potential users test the software before it is commercially released into the market is very critical. The released software should ensure there are no errors and bugs and the software application must work without any problems on any supported system. Beta-testing enables the end-users to test the software to determine if it would satisfy their actual needs.

Prior to conducting beta-testing, the business will perform internal alpha testing to determine whether the software is acceptable to be sent out to potential beta-testers. Users who conduct the beta-testing will enable the business to find out whether the software needs further improvements. Alpha- and beta-tests will also determine whether the software would indeed be useful to potential clients. In essence, beta-testing is a critical procedure that allows the software developers to test their products under field conditions and by the people who will actually use them.

Entities participating in the beta-testing provide specific feedback on both the functionality of the software in terms of meeting user requirements and determine whether the product can withstand the different configurations of the end-user computers, so that the software developer can make improvements before it is released for sale. User opinions can also give software developers a better understanding of the benefits to the user and provide a better understanding as to how the software should be priced when placed for sale in the market, as well as providing more accurate profit projections. Those performing beta-testing typically benefit from a "first look" at software that could potentially improve the efficiency and effectiveness of its own operations. Beta-testing agreements often include provisions that allow the beta-testing entity to use the software at no cost or a discounted price in the future. The potential risk that the beta-testing entity must consider is the potential that a bug in the tested software may have a negative effect on their computer systems. Such risk is typically negotiated and allocated between the parties as part of the Beta-Testing License Agreement. The risk that software developers must consider is that the user will either use or disclose the intellectual property (software) to third parties. Once again the licensing agreement will contain provisions to protect the software developer from such misappropriation.

The initial iCare prototype alpha testing was performed by using three focus groups of students at the University of Tennessee College of Nursing. These students used the iCare system as part of their clinical training to record health care information. The students provided usability feedback to the iCare software developers and changes were made prior to offering the software for outside beta-testing. In planning for beta-testing, Professor Wyatt relied on professional contacts who were interested in obtaining and using EHRs in their own nursing programs. The nursing programs at Kennesaw State University, Shenandoah University, and Kent State University-Stark Campus were selected to participate in the usability study.

However, before the beta-testing could get underway a licensing agreement needed to be drafted to protect the various interests of the parties. Because iCare licensed the software from UTRF, the agreement that would be entered into between iCare and the beta-testing universities would be a Sublicense Agreement. This required clinic student attorneys to draft a document which not only memorialized the agreements made between iCare and the beta-testing university, but also complied with the requirements the original Software License Agreement between iCare and UTRF.

Once the Beta-testing Sublicense Agreement [84] was drafted, the general counsel's office from the participating universities reviewed the agreement to determine if it complied with internal policy and to assess what risks, if any, the universities would be assuming by signing the agreement. Once administrative approval was received, the participating faculty signed the agreement and the software was installed on the beta-testing university hardware, allowing the clinical testing to get underway.

Because Professor Wyatt had expertise in the use of the Nielsen's Usability Model, it was chosen to evaluate the EHR software with the beta-testing focus groups. This model is comprised of five components:

- *Learnability*—How easily can the user learn the product?

- *Efficiency*—How quickly can the user learn the product?

- *Memorability*—Once the user returns to the product, how long will it take to reorient or relearn the product?

- *Errors*—How many errors does the user make?

- *Satisfaction*—How pleasant or unpleasant is the design and functionality and does the product deliver what the user expects?

During the evaluation process involving the focus groups, data collectors allow users to discover mistakes and recover without assistance because this provides more data than simply helping the user. Data collectors do, however, intervene and assist users after it is determined that they can no longer proceed without assistance. Such an evaluation protocol not only improves the functionality of the software, it identifies underlying problems with the software programming.

QUESTIONS

1. What is intellectual property?

2. How are innovations primarily protected in the United States?

3. Patent protection was not sought for the iCare software package. Why do you think this was?

4. Who initially owned the iCare innovation?

5. Why didn't the original inventers own their innovation?

6. What is the role of the University of Tennessee Office Research Foundation ("UTRF")?

7. What did the UTRF decide to do with the iCare innovation and why?

8. How was this accomplished?

9. What, essentially, did this the software licensing agreement do?

10. What is beta-testing?

11. What legal arrangement was necessary before beta-testing of the iCare software package could begin?

CHAPTER 4

SALE OF THE BUSINESS: THE EVALUATION AND PREPARATION STAGES

I. OVERVIEW

The primary focus of the iCare founders was to develop a cost effective EHR software package that could be used as a teaching tool in the nursing program. All of the individuals who worked on the development of the package were academics who were interested in other pursuits beyond the commercialization of iCare as an ongoing business. Thus, capitalizing on the iCare technology would require (1) obtaining expert advice, (2) extensive preparation of business information, and (3) determining the value of the business.

II. OBTAINING EXPERT ADVICE

Although there were opportunities to expand the use of the iCare EHR software package to other nursing schools and healthcare providers, the founders lacked the time, expertise, and experience to accomplish that expansion. So they decided to form an Advisory Board, comprised of individuals with business experience to counsel them on the necessary steps to explore opportunities to monetize the iCare technology. Although the board members were uncompensated volunteers, the student attorneys advised the founders that they should have each of them to sign a nondisclosure and confidentiality agreement so that the advisors would clearly understand the importance of the proprietary nature of the EHR software. Even inadvertent disclosure of information to a third party may jeopardize the value of the technology if a competitor were able to use that information to their advantage. As a result, the student attorneys drafted a Nondisclosure and Advisory Board Member Agreement. [33]

After participating in several strategy sessions with the Advisory Board, the founders concluded that the best opportunity to profit from the development of iCare beyond its use in the classroom was to find another company that already had a presence in the healthcare education market that would be interested in acquiring the technology. They decided to seek the advice of a business acquisition expert who not only understood the health care industry, but who could instruct the team on the steps needed to prepare the business for an acquisition of its assets. They enlisted the services of Rich Berube, who was willing to work with iCare as a consultant on a deferred compensation basis. Because iCare was working with a minimal operating budget, the parties entered into a consulting agreement [87] whereby Berube would work for a fixed yearly salary, but would be paid only if and when the company or its assets were sold to a purchasing party. This is called a "contingency arrangement."

III.   PREPARING iCARE BUSINESS INFORMATION FOR THE SALE

Berube explained to the founders that one of the most daunting aspects of selling a business is the preparation. For entrepreneurs, the need to further develop and run the business far outweighs the required time to gather due diligence items.[1] Advance preparation of a long list of tasks, however, is key to selling a business. Because buyers each emphasize their own business metrics when assessing a potential acquisition, it is best for an entrepreneur to organize all available data for easy access during the early stages of, or even before, the sales transaction process. Preparing the business for a sale or an acquisition is formidable, but taking the time to prepare upfront would allow the founders to gather this information over time, rather than scrambling when the time comes. The majority of businesses are sold (on the impetus of the business owners), rather than bought (on the impetus of a buyer), but if a potential buyer does make inquiries, a business that has spent the time properly documenting its strategy and progress toward well-defined objectives will be more likely to provide the proper impression to a potential buyer. Fortunately, from the very beginning of the iCare matter, the

---

[1]   "Due diligence" or, simply, "diligence," is the process of systematically researching and verifying the accuracy of a statement. The term originated in the business world, where due diligence is required to validate financial statements. The goal of the process is to ensure that all stakeholders associated with a financial endeavor have the information they need to assess risk accurately.

student attorneys emphasized the need to formally document all corporate actions and legally binding rights, privileges, duties, and agreements.

One of the first things potential buyers look at are the company's financial statements. Understanding the value of a potential acquisition is key. Buyers typically look closely at items such as:

- *Revenue*—money that a company actually receives during a specific period, including discounts and deductions for returned merchandise. It is the gross income figure from which costs are subtracted to determine net income. Revenue is calculated by multiplying the price at which goods or services are sold by the number of units or amount sold.

- *Growth*—a company that generates significant positive cash flows or earnings, which increase at significantly faster rates than the overall economy.

- *Gross Margin*—the percent of total sales revenue that the company retains after incurring the direct costs associated with producing the goods and services sold by a company. In other words, a company's total sales revenue minus its cost of goods sold, divided by the total sales revenue, expressed as a percentage.

- *Operating Expenses*—an expenditure that a business incurs as a result of performing its normal business operations.

- *Cash Flow*—a company's cash receipts minus its cash payments—Often expressed as Earnings Before Interest, Taxes Depreciation, and Amortization (EBITDA).

Because iCare was not yet an operating business with customers and sales, Berube advised the founders to prepare financial statements to demonstrate how well the business had used the resources from the founders' personal financial contributions, SBIR grants, and other resources to develop the EHR software package. He encouraged them to provide as much information as possible so that there would be complete transparency. This meant that in addition to an overview of cash in-flows and out-flows, all underlying business records that provide supporting detail as to how such financial resources were obtained and used should be available for a buyer to review. In addition, the documents of interest to a potential buyer included iCare's Articles of Organization [2], Operating Agreement [8], Resolutions and Actions Taken by Written Consent [21]. This level of transparency allows the purchaser to clearly understand the decision-making history of the business, as well as the ownership interests of the members, and their respective roles and responsibilities within the company. The founders decided that they would create a website—with limited, password-protected access—so that they could present this information readily to a buyer, once iCare and the buyer entered into an appropriate confidentiality agreement.

The purpose of having the buyer sign a confidentiality agreement is to protect the seller from the disclosure of the company's intellectual property that the buyer may misappropriate or disclose to a third party that would have the effect of decreasing the value of the business. If both the buyer and the seller will be revealing confidential information, for instance when the purchase price is dependent on the acquired business's future performance, a mutual nondisclosure agreement [34] should be used.

IV. DETERMINING THE VALUE OF THE BUSINESS

The valuation of a business is the process of determining the current worth of a business, using objective measures and evaluating all aspects of the business. A business valuation might include an analysis of the company's management, its capital structure, and its future earnings prospects, as well as the market value or replacement cost of its assets. One of the reasons business valuation is such a complicated issue is because there are many acceptable valuation methods. Rather than using a "one-size-fits-all" valuation approach, sellers need to decide which method is right for their business based on industry, size, and the circumstances of the sale. By definition, startups don't have a history of financial performance on which to base a valuation. Therefore, it's up to the founders to develop a process for valuing the company based on comparable companies and financial projections. This is accomplished by researching how much companies in the same industry and geography are worth.

Valuation can make or break a business sale, because for many sellers attaching a dollar value to their company is a touchy subject—especially if they have spent years building it from a fledgling start-up. Left unchecked, the valuation process can quickly devolve into a pricing routine that is rooted in personal attachments and other subjective inputs rather than solid data based on marketplace realities. The actual value of a start-up business is the amount someone is willing to pay for it in the business-for-sale marketplace. Personal feelings about the company's worth are far less important than sound valuation methodology, accurate documentation, and other factors that could potentially influence value.

Because young businesses take time to become profitable, the key to valuing startups is to focus on the future. First, determine how many years it will take for the business to be profitable. A business with a long road to profitability will usually be worth less than one with a quick path to profitability. Next, determine how much comparable companies have been valued at when they reached profitability. A company that could be worth $5 million at profitability will be worth some fraction of that number at the startup stage, based on factors such as the likelihood of success, the amount of additional investment required, the time frame to exit, the quality of the management team, and the prospective buyer's discount rate or internal rate of return hurdle rate. It is easy to get caught up in the excitement of valuing a company at the highest amount possible and forget that one day a buyer is going to question the underlying assumptions that would be made and challenge the valuation.

Because the most persuasive valuations are objective and analytically sound, the founders considered retaining an independent valuation expert to guide the company through the valuation process. However, because of the rapid interest in the iCare EHR software package, the founders did not end up retaining a valuation consultant. As a result of presentations that Professor Wyatt was making at professional conferences concerning the development of the iCare software and the value of the EHR simulation had in the classroom, a number of schools began making inquiries as to how they could acquire the software. This quickly drew the attention of publishing companies that provided educational materials to nursing and medical schools. Two publishing companies showed particular interest in the software and met with the founders to discuss the possible acquisition of their innovation.

The interest by the publishing companies helped in the valuation process because these companies recognized the value of the iCare product in the market place, and began the process of quantifying how much it would cost and how long it would take to develop their own software from scratch. Purchasing iCare would have several advantages. First, it was developed by academics who possessed both the theoretical and practical experience in the use of EHRs. They developed the software package to use in their own classroom, so it would have a natural appeal to others in the academic community. Second, the iCare EHR software package had already gone through the beta-testing process and as such, had most of the bugs worked out. The founders had spent a considerable amount of time working on the concept, even before they had established iCare as a business entity. Replicating that sort of practical and academic insight into a set of user requirements and then focusing the programming support necessary to fully develop the software would delay entry into the marketplace.

Indeed, one of the reasons the founders embarked upon the project was that purchasing an existing EHR system for use in the classroom was cost prohibitive. The publishing companies knew the going price rates for existing systems in the marketplace and could forecast with some accuracy the demand that existed in the nursing and medical school communities for such a product. The publishing companies also saw the potential for having follow-on sales to medical practices, once those nursing and medical school students graduated. The publishing company executives believed that once a student was trained on a particular EHR system, they would naturally gravitate toward that system if it were offered for use in the practice setting. Once the development costs were quantified, the potential market assessed, and the price point determined for sale of the product to the academic community, the companies were in a good position to discuss the possibility of purchasing the EHR technology from iCare.

Prior to engaging in conversations with either of the publishing companies, the founders met with the student attorneys to have them draft a nondisclosure and confidentiality agreement [34] that would provide them some protection against anyone using the discussions as a pretense to finding out about details of the system and then using that information for their own benefit. Both companies indicated that they would sign such an agreement and that they would like it to be a mutual nondisclosure and confidentiality agreement because both parties would be disclosing proprietary information as part of the sale of the business.

QUESTIONS

1.   Why was a sale of the iCare business the best way for the founders to capitalize on the iCare EHR software package?

2.   What steps must be taken in preparing business information in anticipation of a sale?

3.   What additional action did the iCare founders take in preparing business information?

4. Why have potential buyers enter into a confidentiality agreement?

5.   How are businesses evaluated?

6.   How should young businesses be evaluated?

7.   Did the iCare founders retain a valuation expert? Why or why not?

CHAPTER 5

SALE OF THE BUSINESS: THE NEGOTIATION PROCESS

I. OVERVIEW

The purchase and sale of a business ultimately depends on negotiations. An effective negotiation is one where both parties clearly articulate their expectations and concerns. Ideally, the founders and members of iCare would attempt to create a competitive market by getting more than one company interested in the purchase. But ultimately, there was only one potential suitor that was actively pursuing the iCare acquisition—the academic publishing company, Wolters Kluwer Health, Inc. ("WKH"), which opened the negotiation process by sending iCare a Letter of Intent or ("LOI"). This left iCare at a negotiating disadvantage because they did not have multiple offers to consider and they did not have an independent valuation conducted. However, iCare did have the product that WKH wanted. Thus both parties were in a position to negotiate.

II. THE LETTERS OF INTENT

WKH provided iCare with a LOI [35] dated May 27, 2010, to start off the negotiation process. The purpose of the LOI is to facilitate the start of the business transaction by identifying the critical business and contractual terms which will form the basis of the final contract. The LOI allows the parties to outline the essential terms of the agreement before spending significant time conducting due diligence, obtaining third party approvals, and negotiating definitive agreements. Because the purpose of the LOI is to provide a framework for further negotiations, it is intended to be non-binding. However, if the parties fail to state the intent for the LOI to be nonbinding, it is generally presumed to be binding and enforceable by the courts. Also, courts may infer intent for the LOI to be binding from subsequent conduct and communications between the parties.

Even nonbinding LOIs can have binding features. Many LOIs contain binding provisions such as: governing law; non-disclosure and confidentiality; and covenants for exclusivity in negotiation rights and good faith in negotiations between the parties. If properly negotiated, the LOI can protect both parties. For example, the buyer may want to be able to discontinue the purchase in the event that they cannot obtain satisfactory financing. The seller may want the LOI to contain a non-solicitation provision, preventing the potential purchaser from hiring the seller's employees in the event the transaction does not go through.

The WKH LOI [93] that was offered to iCare on May 27, 2010, was very comprehensive. It clearly indicated that WKH did not want to buy the LLC, only certain of its assets.[1] The LOI also sketched out

---

[1]   An asset sale is the purchase of individual assets and liabilities, whereas a stock sale is the purchase of the owner's shares of a corporation. While there are many considerations when negotiating the type of transaction, tax implications and potential

the general parameters of the purchase price, including: reimbursement of development and operating costs up to $300,000, an upfront cash payment of $500,000, and a 15% annual royalty on gross revenue beginning in 2011, with a guaranteed minimum annual royalty payments of $250,000 in 2012 and 2013. The LOI was offered as a basis for negotiation for the "possible" acquisition of assets, and was contingent upon the satisfactory completion of the due diligence process and the negotiation and execution of mutually satisfactory final documentation including an asset purchase agreement. The LOI also contained a provision requiring exclusive negotiating rights for a designated period of time—until July 31, 2010. The LOI was set to expire at 5:00 pm Central time on June 4, 2010 if it was not signed and returned before that time.

A. INITIAL CONCERNS OF THE ICARE FOUNDERS

Prior to entering into negotiation with WKH, the founders needed to meet and determine whether they should sign the LOI, which would bind iCare to negotiating the terms of a sale in good faith based on

---

liabilities are the primary concerns. If the business in question is a sole proprietorship, a partnership, or a limited liability company (LLC), the transaction cannot be structured as a stock sale since none of these entity structures have stock. Instead, owners of these entity types can sell their partnership or membership interests as opposed to the entity selling its assets. If the business is incorporated, either as a regular C-corporation or as a sub-S corporation, the buyer and seller must decide whether to structure the deal as an asset sale or a stock sale.

WKH's proposal. Because iCare was a limited liability company, everyone who held a membership interest in the entity had a vote on any potential sale, including UTRF.[2] The iCare operating agreement [8] required that a majority of the membership interests must vote to approve the sale, transfer, exchange, or lease of any of the company's property. While all the members were in general agreement that they wanted to monetize the value that they had in the development of the EHR system, there were many details of the transaction that were not clear to the members.

The iCare founders consulted with their business acquisitions expert, Rich Berube, and student attorneys who explained the contents of the LOI, the issues that needed further clarification, and the information that needed to be collected and provided to the purchaser. Berube explained that the purchaser was offering to buy iCare's assets and not the business entity. This would benefit the buyer because it could purchase the assets of the iCare that it needed to obtain all the rights in the EHR system's intellectual property without buying any of iCare's liabilities. An asset purchase would also allow the purchaser to allocate the purchase price among the assets to reflect their fair market value, with certain tax implications. This would result in a step-up tax basis (the adjustment of the value of an appreciated asset for tax purposes), and allow higher depreciation

---

[2]   As part of the licensing agreement with the iCare founders, UTRF took a 10% ownership interest in the limited liability company.

and amortization deductions, which would result in future federal tax savings. The only other alternative to an asset sale would be for the members to sell their individual membership interests in iCare to the purchaser, but this could prove to be more cumbersome and there would be little advantage for either of the parties to structure the sale in this fashion.

The heart of the discussion centered on the purchase price, which was broken down into four primary components:

1. WKH would reimburse iCare for its development and operating costs up to $300,000, upon the showing of appropriate invoices for such costs and services;

2. iCare would receive $500,000 in January 2011, after closing the transaction;

3. iCare would receive a 15% annual royalty payment commencing in 2011 on the gross revenues (less bad debt and returns) from sales of the iCare product. In the years 2012 and 2013, iCare would be guaranteed a minimum annual royalty payment of $250,000, contingent upon the iCare founders providing certain specified consulting services (at no additional cost). In the event that the consulting services were not provided, the royalty payments would be reduced by an

amount to be determined in the final documentation.[3]

Essentially, WKH was willing to pay iCare approximately $1,300,000, with future royalties unaddressed for the product. iCare's major concerns were:

- The terms of the purchase price set out in the LOI. Although the members developed the EHR system primarily for use in their classroom and had no interest in growing the business on their own, they thought their product was worth more, and wanted a higher royalty rate and more guaranteed royalty payments. They were also aware that there was a finite time or window during which the iCare EHR system would be marketable.

- The rights and scope-of-use the university would have of the iCare product after the purchase. The university owned the rights in the EHR system, which was created with federal funds by university employees and students. As a result, the university could

---

[3] This provision in the letter of intent is similar to an earn-out provision. This sort of pricing structure limits the risk of the buyer so that future purchase payments are contingent upon future revenues from the sales of the product, and, in this case, cooperation with the founders in providing certain consulting services in the further development of the EHR system. In the event that the iCare product proved to be more successful in the marketplace than was anticipated by the purchasing company, the members could enjoy the benefits of such success in that there was potential to earn more in royalty payments than the $250,000 guaranteed minimum payments.

only grant the purchaser a license to use the product and the university would need to have a perpetual, systemwide use of the EHR system after it was acquired.

- How much time were the members expected to spend providing consulting services, and when would those services need to be performed? Given that the founders had full time obligations with the University of Tennessee, negotiations needed to focus on what consulting services were required, and how much time the university would allow them to participate in such activities. In addition, if the members were required to travel, would their travel expenses be reimbursed?

- Because so much of the sales price was contingent upon future royalty payments, the members wanted the ability to monitor how royalties and deductions were calculated. Because WKH would have control over when the product was introduced to the market, and would be in exclusive control over the financial data in terms of gross revenues, the members wanted to ensure that a mechanism was in place to ensure compliance with the terms of the agreement.

B.   FURTHER NEGOTIATIONS

Although some of the membership wanted to attempt to pursue interest from other publishing companies to see if they could obtain better offers, they agreed that further negotiation with WKH regarding the LOI was the best course of action.

During the negotiation process, each party is negotiating from the perspective of their own needs and business objectives, and each transaction brings its own set of nuances and circumstances that the other party is not in a position to fully appreciate without further detailed discussions. Both parties should refrain from being offended during this process. They need to understand that this conversation and sharing of otherwise hidden points of interest and objectives is a normal part of the fact-finding and negotiation process that can lead to a more mutually satisfactory agreement.

Here, the iCare members expressed their concerns about the purchase price structure and the University of Tennessee's intellectual use rights. After several weeks of discussions, WKH agreed to: (1) an increased annual royalty of 18% (3% higher than the 15% stated in the LOI), and (2) minimum guaranteed royalty payments for three years: 2012, 2013, and 2014 (one additional year more than set out in the LOI). It appears that both parties recognized there was a finite period in which the iCare product would be marketable, because they agreed that "Payment of any iCare Royalty will only run through December 31, 2015." WKH also agreed to grant the University of Tennessee a royalty-free, non-transferrable license through the end of 2015 to use the iCare product.

WKH provided iCare with an LOI [85] dated June 21, 2010, that contained these changes. However, this LOI was not signed by iCare within the 2-day period before its expiration date of June 23, 2010. That was not the end of the process, however. After the summer, WKH provided iCare with another LOI [86], dated September 7, 2010, that contained the same terms at the June 21 LOI. The members agreed to sign the September 7 LOI and pursue more detailed discussions concerning the above issues. They understood they were binding iCare to an exclusive negotiating period with the purchasing company. The parties progressed to the next stage in the negotiation process: due diligence.

III. DUE DILIGENCE

In this instance, negotiations were greatly enhanced by the level of detail contained in the LOI [86]. When most people think about negotiations, they think about the parties and their attorneys sitting around a conference table discussing the terms of the LOI. However, at this stage of the process, most of the details were discussed over the phone by the members of iCare and the publishing company's business representatives. With the guidance provided by the acquisitions consultant and student attorneys, the members collected invoices and supporting documentation to justify reimbursement for the development and operating costs. The fundamental documentation that was provided to WKH as part of this process was:

- Entity legal documentation, including articles of organization [2], operating agreements [8], resolutions and actions taken upon written consent [21];

• Licensing agreements between the University of Tennessee [32], UTRF, and iCare [31];

• Financing documents that included promissory notes [23] associated with the personal loans provided by the founders and the SBIR grant [27] provided by the federal government;

• EHR program, source code, and user manual;

• Beta-testing results and evaluations;

• Accounting, federal and state tax records; and

• Service and consulting [22] contracts [87].

Due diligence greatly contributes to the negotiation and decision making process. The representatives of WKH were given demonstrations on how the EHR system was used in the classroom. However, providing all the possible information about the system to allow WKH's information technology specialists an opportunity to analyze all of the details of the product gives further assurances that the system will perform as demonstrated. It also provides insight into all of the potential costs, benefits, and risks associated with future commercialization of the system. As one can imagine, this analysis cannot be accomplished overnight and may require some further detailed discussions with the members, as well as the contract service providers that participated in the development of the system.[4]

After many weeks of due diligence and discussions, both parties were in a position to move on to the next phase of the asset purchase process—drafting the asset purchase agreement or APA.

QUESTIONS

1. How did the negotiation process begin in the iCare matter?

2. What is a Letter of Intent or LOI?

3. What were important provisions of the WKH LOI?

4. What were the iCare members' concern regarding the May 27, 2010, LOI?

5. What did iCare do as part of the due diligence portion of the negotiation process?

6. What was the result of the negotiation process regarding this LOI?

7. Why wasn't the June 21, 2010, LOI signed by iCare when they were willing to sign the September 7, 2010, LOI with the same terms?

---

[4]　As part of the due diligence process, iCare was providing essentially all of the information concerning its intellectual property to the WKH. Since the EHR system was not patented, in the absence of the signed mutual confidentiality agreement there would be no assurances that the purchasing company could not discontinue negotiations and use the information they learned to create their own system.

CHAPTER 6

SALE OF THE BUSINESS: DRAFTING THE ASSET PURCHASE AGREEMENT

I. OVERVIEW

The purpose of the asset purchase agreement (the "APA") is to describe the assets of the business to be purchased; document the nature of the transaction between the parties; define the representations (statements and promises) made by each party in relation to the sale; define closing conditions; assign or allocate risks in the transaction between the buyer and seller; and provide a timetable and path for closing the transaction.

Four sets of attorneys were involved in drafting the iCare APA:

- WKH's inside corporate counsel;

- WKH's outside counsel that had expertise in acquisitions and licensing matters;

- UTRF's outside counsel that had expertise in acquisitions and licensing matters; and

- iCare's student attorneys.

WKH wanted its outside counsel to take the lead in drafting the APA and supporting documentation because they had represented purchasing companies in prior transactions of this nature and thus were familiar with the form and content of what was required. This would save time and legal fees in the drafting process because they would have exemplars from the previous transactions that could be employed in documenting the present transaction.

Typically, the purchasing company takes the lead on drafting the asset purchase agreement so that they have control over the substance and form that the agreement takes. From a strategic standpoint, the parties drafting the agreements place themselves in a superior bargaining position by having their version of the various provisions down on paper first, so that the other party is forced to react to the positions taken. The selling company will not always agree with the proposed provisions and it should be expected that through further negotiations they will arrive on language less burdensome to the seller.[1] In this case, UTRF and iCare student attorneys would then react to the details of the draft through the mark-up process.

Drafting the APA is accomplished through the use of a fairly logical and standardized format. However, all transactions are not "standard" and, as such, the format may need to be altered, depending on the type of business, scope, size, and complexity of the transaction. For example, an agreement for the sale of a manufacturing company will contain representations and warranties that may be quite different than those of a software company such as

---

[1]   See George W. Kuney, The Elements of Contract Drafting: With Questions and Clauses for Consideration 38 (4th ed. 2014). [36]

iCare. The iCare APA used the following documentation structure.

II. RECITALS [37]

Recitals are situated at the beginning of the agreement and are also referred to as an introduction or preamble.[2] They provide a general idea about the contract to its reader such as: what the contract is about, who the parties are, why they are signing the contract, and the date of the agreement. The recitals are also known as the "Whereas Clauses" because of the somewhat antiquated practice of starting each with the word "Whereas," which can safely be abandoned by modern drafters. The recitals do not contain rights and obligations of the parties, but merely explain or introduce the nature of or background to the agreement. The recitals are followed by the substantive provisions of the agreement structured in an "Article" and "Section" format.

III. ARTICLE I—DEFINITIONS [38]

The purpose of the definition section is to provide clarity and consistency in the application of terms used throughout the agreement.[3] Defined terms can decrease the length and increase the readability of subsequent substantive sections. Defined terms are listed in alphabetical order for ease of reference.

---

2   *Id.* at 31. [39]

3   *Id.* at 32. [40]

Defined terms that are used in only one section should be defined when they are used. When defined as used in a section, the defined term should *also* be included in the master definition section, using the phrase: " **'Term'** has the meaning set forth in **Section**—." The purpose of including the sectional definition within the master definitional list is to ensure that if the definition is changed, that change will ripple through the document automatically and avoid the ambiguity that could occur by revising the definition in one appearance of the agreement and not in another. Defined terms, when used in the body of the agreement, are often used in **boldface** or Initial Capitals, as are all cross references to **Articles**, **Sections** and **Schedules**.

IV.   ARTICLE II—PURCHASE AND SALE OF ASSETS [41]

This article is the heart of the asset purchase transaction. It identifies the assets that were transferred, the liabilities assumed, and the payment structure for those assets. In the iCare APA, **Purchase and Sales of Assets, Section 2.1** [41] identifies the assets to be purchased in a general fashion. These assets were identified as part of WKH's due diligence process. In essence, WKH acquired all of iCare's assets used or held for use in its business, including intellectual property, as well as certain contracts. The APA then referenced several schedules that listed the specific assets that would be acquired or excluded from the purchase.

- Schedule 2.1(a)(ii) [42] lists the Acquired
  Contracts

- Schedule 2.1(a)(v) [43] lists the Acquired
  Intellectual Property

- Schedule 2.1(b)(vii) [44] lists the Excluded
  Contracts

- Schedule 2.1(b)(xi) [45] lists the Excluded
  Assets

The use of schedules that are incorporated by
reference into the APA allows the reader to see the
specific list of assets that will be included in the
purchase, as well as which assets will be excluded,
without being overshadowed by the density of the
legal language within the agreement itself.[4] Even if
there are no assets of intellectual property that are
being excluded, a schedule may still be included,
stating "None." This provides even further clarity of
the parties' intent that all assets and intellectual
property with the exclusion of certain contracts
would be part of the APA.

The same is true with **Assumed and Excluded
Liabilities, Section 2.2** [47]. For the buyer, one of
the key benefits of an asset purchase compared to a
stock purchase transaction is that in a stock
purchase, the whole company is being obtained along
with all of its assets and liabilities. In the case of the
iCare asset purchase transaction, WKH was willing
to assume only a very narrow set of extraordinary
liabilities that arose out of closing. Those specific

---

[4]   *Id.* at 36. [46]

liabilities that were identified as part of the due diligence process were enumerated in **Schedule 2.2(b)** [48]. The listed excluded liabilities dealt with the outstanding personal loans provided by the founders, deferred payments associated with consulting contracts, and any potential amounts due under a service contract in relation to programming support. The body of **Section 2.2** lists a comprehensive exclusion of liabilities (some that did not even apply to the operational circumstances of iCare) in the event that items were missed by WKH during the due diligence process.

The **Purchase Price; Royalties Section 2.3** [49], was a section that required a great deal of additional refinement during the drafting process because of the concerns expressed by iCare following negotiations over the LOI. The payment of iCare's operating and development costs were substantiated through the prior provision of invoices and were listed separately in **Schedule 2.3(a)** [50]. The reimbursement of such costs were capped at $300,000, and were to be paid at closing.

The other agreed upon purchase price and royalty payments were further defined both in timing and method of payment. The following payments were to be made by bank wire transfer to an account specified by the seller, iCare:

- The purchase price of $500,000 would be paid on January 31, 2011,[5]

---

[5]   The payment of the purchase price was delayed until the start of the fiscal year for tax reasons. Generally, sellers prefer to

- The 2011 iCare Royalty payment would be paid no later than April 1, 2012,[6]

- The 2012 Guarantee Amount royalty payment would be paid no later than February 15, 2013, and the excess of the iCare Royalty over the Guarantee Amount would be paid not later than April 1, 2013,

- The 2013 Guarantee Amount royalty payment would be paid no later than February 15, 2014, and the excess of the iCare Royalty over the Guarantee Amount would be paid not later than April 1, 2014,

- The 2014 Guarantee Amount royalty payment would be paid no later than February 15, 2015, and the excess of the iCare Royalty over the Guarantee Amount would be paid not later than April 1, 2015,

- The 2015 royalty payment would be paid no later than February 15, 2016.

Title II Definitions [38] defined "iCare Royalty" as "the product of 18% and that calendar year's gross revenues (less bad debts and returns), and "Guarantee Amount" as "$250,000." Therefore, for fiscal years 2012, 2013, and 2014, minimum royalty

---

defer taxable events such as receipt of payment if it is near the end of the tax year, while buyers often want to accelerate them so that they can use the payment as a deductible business expense, which will decrease their taxes in the current year.

6   The royalty payments were delayed for a period of time considered necessary to accurately account for calculation of gross revenues (less bad debt and returns).

payments of $250,000 would be paid. If royalties exceeded this base amount, additional payments would be made based upon 18% gross revenues (less bad debt and returns). For fiscal year 2015, there would be no guaranteed royalty payments and iCare would receive only the actual royalties earned.

The royalty payments could also be reduced in the event that the iCare founders did not provide certain specified consulting services necessary to further develop the iCare product. This was a major concern for iCare. As full time faculty and students, their consulting duties had to comply with both university policy, as well as availability of personal time to accomplish the work. The student attorneys representing iCare needed to negotiate with WKH's attorneys to draft a mechanism for accomplishing the designated consulting services that addressed WKH's needs yet allowed flexibility for the iCare founders to meet the obligations they had to the University of Tennessee.

This was a major issue in moving the deal forward. iCare's founders did not want to proceed with the transaction with so much uncertainty on what was to be expected of them in terms of workload and timing of work to be accomplished. They did not want to be in the position of entering into the agreement and losing all the potential royalty payments due to their inability to accomplish the consulting services within the time frame expected by WKH. In turn, WKH did not want to embark upon an effort to bring the EHR system to market without the timely support necessary from the iCare founders. After lengthy discussions, the parties agreed to an approach that both parties understood and that appeared to be workable. The attorneys worked together to draft documents that provided a framework to accomplish the work required within reasonable time frames, while accommodating the iCare founders' university work obligations. WKH also compromised that any royalty reduction would only affect the guaranteed amounts. The attorneys drafted the following documents that working in concert achieved the desired results:

- *Master Consulting Agreement* [51]—Each of the iCare founders entered into a separate consulting agreement that defined the scope of work as independent contractors, and provided that they would be working without compensation as part of the agreed upon terms of the APA.

- *Statement of Work* [52]—The statement of work defined project-specific activities, deliverables, and timelines. The iCare founders worked with the purchasing company business people and information technology personnel to clearly define these parameters.

- *Offset Against iCare Royalties and Guarantee Amounts*—**Schedule 2.3(h)** [53]—provided a 45 cumulative day delay in accomplishing the tasks outlined in the Statement of Work. After that time, the guaranteed payments would be reduced by $1,100 a day beyond the 45th day.

These documents were referenced in **Section 2.3(h)** [53] and included as schedules and Exhibits as part of the "APA Transaction Bible."[7]

Another critical issue for iCare was the length of "Use Rights" proposed in the LOI. WKH proposed to grant the University of Tennessee (Knoxville) a royalty-free, non-transferable license to use the iCare product through the end of 2015. This was proposed to enable professors and researchers at the university to conduct research that would further the development of the iCare product. Even though the founders of iCare developed the EHR system, because it was created at the university using federal funds, the university was the true owner of the IP; iCare merely licensed the invention back from the University for the purposes of commercialization. The attorneys representing UTRF insisted that the university should receive a perpetual, royalty-free, non-transferable license to use the iCare product. Not only was this university policy for all IP that was created on campus and subsequently licensed to private industry, but the original purpose for the development of the iCare product was for use in the classroom.

After several weeks of detailed discussions, the parties reached a compromise which would allow "UT, its faculty and its nursing, and other health care and veterinary students" to have a royalty-free, non-

---

[7]   The Transaction Bible is a set of main documents signed in a deal that is grouped together for ease of reference. It usually includes copies of the relevant deal documents. Certain documents may not be included in the bible for confidentiality purposes.

transferable license to use the then-most recent
iCare product. **Section 2.3(i)** [54]. This usage grant
was more particularly described in **Schedule 2.3(i)**
[54]. However, after reviewing the detailed schedule
another issue was presented. It became apparent
that WKH planned on marketing the iCare product
both as a "stand-alone" version and as a "bundled"
version with other printed materials such as text
books. WKH would be offering the bundled version at
a discount to the stand-alone version, if sold
separately. The question arose, how would this effect
the calculation of royalty amounts due to iCare?

Once again, extensive discussions were conducted
to negotiate the detailed terms concerning how
royalties would be calculated when the iCare product
was bundled with other purchasing company
products. WKH explained that they needed flexibility
in terms of determining what the best and most cost-
effective manner in which to market the iCare
product. The founders expressed their concern that
any discounts of the iCare product when bundled
would decrease the amount of royalties they would
receive. The parties finally reached a detailed
compromise. Because these details required both a
mathematical and written explanation on how
royalties would be calculated, the drafters were
concerned that such a lengthy description within the
APA itself could prove confusing. As a result, it was
decided that a separate exhibit should be drafted and
attached to the APA as **Exhibit A—Royalty
Calculations** [55].

The final section of Article II, **Section 2.4, Allocation of Purchase Price** [49], dealt with how the purchase price would be accounted for by the parties. From a federal tax perspective, a sale of the assets of a business is treated as if there were a number of sales of individual assets. **Section 2.4** represents the agreement between WKH and iCare as to how the aggregate purchase price is allocated among the specific assets to be purchased. The purpose of this agreement is to assure that both buyer and seller are consistent in their reporting of the transaction for tax purposes. In this case, the parties agreed to coordinate the purchase allocation of the purchase price prior to submission of the information to the Internal Revenue Service.[8] Such an agreement on allocation is important because, in most asset transactions involving the sale of an entire business, the parties will have to comply with the Internal Revenue Code for reporting such transactions.[9]

---

[8]   The asset purchase agreement provides how the purchase price will be allocated among the assets for tax purposes. The parties may have different objectives when it comes to the allocation of purchase price for tax reporting purposes. For example, sellers may prefer allocations to assets that generate capital gain which receive preferential tax treatment and buyers prefer allocations to assets that generate depreciation and amortization deductions. In the iCare transaction, the parties agreed to coordinate the reporting of the purchase price and certain other costs among the assets.

[9]   Internal Revenue Code § 1060 [56] requires the buyer and the seller to file IRS Form 8594 [57] (Asset Acquisition Statement under Section 1060), describing the allocation with their returns for the year in which there was a transfer of assets used in a trade or business if (a) any good will or going concern value could attach to any of the assets and (b) the buyer's basis in the assets is

V. ARTICLE III—CLOSING

The purpose of the provision on closing is to establish a time, place, and method for the asset sales agreement to be signed along with all supporting documents necessary for effective consummation of the transaction. Setting the date for closing depends upon the complexity of the transaction and the interests of the parties to complete the transaction within a specific time frame. There are a number of factors that may influence the closing date. For example, the purchasing company may need time to complete due diligence or obtain financing. There are also tax, accounting, and practical reasons for scheduling a closing. The selling company may not want to schedule closing on a Friday if they could not have use of the funds over the weekend. This is particularly a concern with financially large transactions where it is crucial to properly schedule the time of day closing should take place so that a wire transfer could be made in time to allow the bank to invest the funds overnight. Often, a physical inventory needs to be conducted prior to closing and the inventory needs to be undertaken during a time where it will have minimal impact on operations.

In some transactions, the closing section contains a list of deliverables and the closing obligations of the parties. In the iCare transaction, the closing article

---

determined wholly by the amount paid for the assets. Compliance with § 1060 will also require disclosure of the consideration paid for employment or consulting agreements with shareholders of the seller who previously were key employees. MODEL ASSET PURCHASE AGREEMENT § 5 cmt., at 52 (Am. Bar. Assoc. ed., 2001).

was very concise, preferring to include all of the closing deliverables in Article VII—Closing Deliveries [58]. WKH contemplated an electronic exchange of documents between the parties followed by an exchange of copies of the original executed documents soon after closing.[10] This allowed the parties to virtually close the transaction, rather than requiring them to meet at one physical location.

VI.   ARTICLES IV AND V— REPRESENTATIONS AND WARRANTIES

Representations and warranties are one of the most heavily negotiated provisions in an asset sales transaction. Representations are statements of past or existing facts, and warranties are promises that those past or existing facts are or will be true.[11] Representations are meant to give one party some reassurance that the other party's statements of fact

---

[10]   Historically, closings occurred in person with representatives of both parties and their counsel present. It is now common practice, however, to complete closings by phone, fax, e-mail, and/or wire transfer without an in-person meeting. The electronic exchange of documents is facilitated by **Article IX, Section 9.8 Counterparts** [59]. "This Agreement may be executed in one or more counterparts, each of which will be deemed to be an original copy of the Agreement and all of which, when taken together, will be deemed to constitute one and the same agreement." This clause permits the agreement to be executed in multiple, identical, copies, when, for example, the parties do not sign the document in the same location. The counterpart clause makes it clear that each party need not sign the same copy of the document in order to have a legally enforceable agreement.

[11]   *See generally* GEORGE W. KUNEY, THE ELEMENTS OF CONTRACT DRAFTING: WITH QUESTIONS AND CLAUSES FOR CONSIDERATION 81 (4th ed. 2014). [60]

are true. They effectively shift the risk that a stated fact is untrue to the representing party.[12]

Article IV—Representations and Warranties of the Seller [61]

The seller's representations are generally much longer and more detailed than the buyer's. The buyer's assessment of the transaction depends on facts that the seller is in the best position to know about and disclose—the seller is what economists would call the "least-cost provider" of this information. Representations are thus also used to shift the burden in the due diligence process.

For example, rather than requiring the buyer to go through a rigorous and comprehensive due diligence process investigating the representations made, the buyer may propose that the seller merely provide a blanket or unqualified representation. This has the effect of shifting the burden of investigation and disclosure back on the seller which is more efficient, as they are the least-cost provider of the information. The representations and warranties serve three primary purposes from the buyer's perspective:

- They further the due diligence process by identifying problems or issues with the seller's business or assets so they can be addressed

---

[12]   If a representation is found to be untrue, remedies may exist in tort for fraud or in contract for breach of implied warranty, breach of express warranty (if the description is basic to the agreement), and rescission. If a provision is merely a warranty and not a representation, only damages for breach are available, not rescission. These basic common-law rules regarding remedies may be modified by local law or by the contract itself.

before an agreement is signed or taken into account in arriving at a purchase price. If these issues cannot be resolved through negotiation, the parties may terminate the transaction;

• They allow the buyer to sign the purchase agreement when the closing is scheduled for a later date (as opposed to simultaneous signing and closing) and walk away from the transaction without closing if the buyer learns that the representations are not accurate at closing; and

• They serve as a basis for allowing the buyer to recover some of its purchase price through indemnification[13] after closing if the seller's representations are inaccurate and the buyer incurs damages.

Although WKH conducted a fairly comprehensive due diligence process in the iCare transaction, they drafted a blanket representation and warranties section [61]. The rationale was that they were relying solely on the materials that were provided by iCare, and in the event items or issues were overlooked, they would be protected. During the mark-up process, the iCare student attorneys attempted to

---

[13]   The representations and warranties provided by a seller in an acquisition agreement create the basic structure for allocating risk between a buyer and a seller. The foundation of that structure is the strength of the indemnification provision, which enforces those representations and warranties. The seller's indemnification provision in the iCare transaction is located within **Article VIII— Survival; Indemnification; Limited Recourse, Section 8.2**. [62]

limit the scope of the representations and warranties as much as they could. They did this by editing the purchasing company's draft, qualifying the representation or warranty by what the seller knew at the time of sale,[14] and also by qualifying what items were material and what would cause a materially adverse effect.[15]

Some of the representations that WKH included in their first draft dealt with easily obtainable items such as whether iCare LLC was in good legal standing with the state of Tennessee and that the members authorized the sale of the assets. Because the iCare student attorneys were confident that these

---

[14]   A seller wants "knowledge" to be defined as actual knowledge so that there is no investigation requirement and no uncertainty as to the application of the standard. Often, an agreement will merely use the term "knowledge" without defining it. This can create disputes after closing that the parties could avoid by using a more precise definition. For example, in the case of iCare the knowledge definition was very specific, naming each of the individuals who were to be expected to have knowledge based upon the scope of their respective job responsibilities. Rather than an actual knowledge standard, iCare agreed to be held to what a prudent individual would be aware of in the course of performing their duties or responsibilities within the scope of their job responsibilities.

[15]   Material Adverse Effect (also referred to as material adverse event or material adverse change) means any result, occurrence, fact, change, event or effect that has, or could reasonably be expected to have, a materially adverse effect on the business, assets, liabilities, capitalization, condition, results of operations, or prospects of the company being purchased. The provision is often found in asset purchase or merger and acquisition agreements and enables the buyer to refuse to complete the acquisition with the seller or, depending how the provision is drafted, allow for compensation after completing the transaction.

representations were accurate, there was no need to negotiate for further qualifications.

Some of the representations, however, required the student attorneys to coordinate with the members of iCare who developed the software to be sure that the representations contained in **Section 4.10 Intellectual Property** [63] were accurately drafted and that there was no intellectual property such as trademarks, internet domain names, and copyrights that were not listed in **Schedule 4.10(a)(i)** [64], which listed all of the intellectual property that was being sold in the transaction. During this process the student attorneys discovered that two domain names were omitted from the list. The same was true with the representations contained **Section 4.11 Material Contracts** [65]—after going through the files, the student attorneys discovered that the agreements with other universities that participated in the beta-testing phase of the iCare product development had not been disclosed. These items were then added to **Schedule 4.11(a) Material Contracts** [66].

The mark-up process of the representations and warranties section also required the student attorneys to coordinate with the attorneys for UTRF, as there was a need for assurances that there was agreement on the language of the representations in terms of licensing and other agreements that were entered into between iCare and UTRF. Although UTRF had a 10% membership interest in iCare and would share in the proceeds of the sales of the iCare product, UTRF attorneys also had a duty to represent

UTRF to ensure that all of the university's intellectual property interests and agreements were properly characterized in the transaction. This not only required changes in the language contained in the representation and warranties section, but it required modifying some of the other agreements that were previously entered into between iCare and UTRF, in order to allow the sale to go through.

The remaining representations and warranties [61] pertaining to such items as Employees, Employee Benefit Plans; Government Contracts, Litigation, Compliance with Laws; Permits, Environmental Matters, Solvency, and the like were included in WKH's draft more as a matter of ensuring protection for WKH against a comprehensive list of possible risks that were not identified as part due diligence and negotiations, but are typically encountered in transactions of this kind.

Article V—Representations and Warranties of the Buyer [67]

Compared to the seller's representations and warranties, the buyer's representations were more limited in scope. iCare's primary concern was that WKH had the authority to enter into the asset purchase transaction and that it had sufficient funds to complete the transaction. Because WKH clearly made such assurances, there was no need for extensive negotiation and editing of this section.

VII. ARTICLE VI—COVENANTS [68]

A covenant is a promise to take an action or refrain from taking an action.[16] The purpose of having covenants in an asset purchase agreement is to govern the actions of the parties from pre-closing through post-closing. In the iCare APA there is one pre-closing covenant that applied to both iCare and WKH, **Section 6.1, Further Assurances** [68]. This is a fairly straight forward provision that requires both parties to use commercially reasonable efforts[17] to consummate the transaction. This provision recognizes the fact that in any transaction, no matter how well planned, issues will arise that may impact the anticipated closing date. Despite these issues, the parties will pursue a course of action to close the transaction in a timely fashion, based upon good faith business judgments.

In addition, the parties also agreed to two mutual post-closing covenants:

- **6.5 Assistance and Cooperation** [68], required the exchange of necessary

---

[16] *See generally* George W. Kuney, The Elements of Contract Drafting: With Questions and Clauses for Consideration 97 (4th ed. 2014). [69]

[17] "Commercially reasonable efforts" is a term that is difficult to define with any precision and will vary depending on the context in which it is used. It is based upon a standard of reasonableness, which is a nominally "objective" test of what a reasonable person would do in the individual circumstance, taking all factors into account. Commercially reasonable efforts is a less rigorous standard than "best efforts" clauses contained in some agreements. Commercially reasonable efforts should be viewed within the context of good faith business judgments.

accounting, financial, and tax information for a period of six years. This provision is important to iCare as it would need accounting information to determine whether royalties were properly being made.

- **6.6 Litigation Support** [68], required both parties to cooperate in defending a third-party's claims involving any aspect of the asset sales transaction. The parties will be responsible for their own costs associated with this obligation.

The remaining covenants were post-closing covenants in which iCare agreed to the following terms:

- **Tax Matters** [68]—required iCare to file and pay all taxes for the periods pre-closing and post-closing.

- **Non-Competition; Non-Solicitation** [68]— restricted iCare from competing with and soliciting customers of the purchasing company, subject to the Protocols and License Rights that appear in **Schedule 6.3(b)** [70]. (This type of covenant is sometimes referred to as a restrictive covenant because it restricts action rather than requires an action).

- **Confidentiality** [68]—required iCare to use commercially reasonable efforts to keep secret any confidential or proprietary information of the purchasing company, and the acquired assets, both pre- and post-closing. This provision acts to extend the confidentiality agreement that was introduced at the start of negotiations through the Mutual Non-Disclosure Agreement [34].

- **6.7 Seller's Obligation to Cease Use of Names and Similar Terms** [68]—required iCare and its members to cease using the corporate name iCare, and any trademark, brand name, domain name, or term that would confuse the consuming public as to the source of the assets being purchased.

VIII.   ARTICLE VII—CLOSING DELIVERIES [58]

This article specified the items that need to be exchanged by the parties by the closing date. Since this closing was done virtually, the documents required for closing were sent prior to the closing date so that the parties could review the documents to determine whether they met the expectations of both parties. In some instances, modifications were required to clearly document the intentions of all the parties involved. WKH's attorneys drafted the assignment documents necessary to effectively transfer the intellectual property or IP rights from iCare and the individual members of the company that created the iCare product. As a result, all that was required was for an appointed officer to sign the documents for iCare, and for the individual creators of the IP to sign the documents which assigned any residual individual interest they retained in the IP to

WKH.[18] The individual creators also needed to sign the Master Consulting Agreement [51], agreeing to provide continued consulting support for the continued development of the iCare product.

iCare also needed to provide all executed agreements it had entered into between UT and UTRF concerning the iCare product. This was necessary to provide assurances to WKH that there was nothing contained in those agreements that would hinder the marketing and sale of the iCare product once it was acquired. Finally, iCare's Board of Directors needed to provide a signed certification that the entity was legally formed in the state of Tennessee and that the sale was authorized by the limited liability company's membership through the procedures outlined in iCare's operating agreement [8]. A comprehensive catch-all provision requiring iCare to essentially provide any additional authorization and documentation necessary to convey full title to the acquired assets, was also included in the closing deliveries. Finally, iCare's President, Tami Wyatt, signed the Asset Purchase Agreement [71] itself, finalizing the transaction.

WKH's list of closing deliveries was much less extensive. The primary delivery that iCare was concerned about was the upfront payment of $300,000 for the reimbursement of operating costs,

---

[18]   The deliverables language "duly executed counterpart" allowed the parties to the transaction to sign separate signature pages of the same document at their places of business, which were combined at closing, becomes a legally enforceable agreement. This process is provided for in **Section 9.8 Counterparts** [59].

which would be delivered via wire transfer to iCare's bank account. The remaining deliveries included countersigning the Intellectual Property Assignment [72], Master Consulting Agreement [51], and Intellectual Property License [73], all of which were drafted by WKH. WKH's president and chief executive officer provided a signed signature page counterpart, authorizing the Asset Purchase Agreement.

IX.   ARTICLE VIII—SURVIVAL; INDEMNIFICATION; LIMITED RECOURSE [62]

In order for representations, warranties, covenants, and agreements between the buyer and seller to form the basis for liability after closing, those provisions must survive the closing.[19] In negotiations, the seller would typically like the shortest survival period achievable, while the buyer wants the longest possible survival period. Covenants and agreements typically survive indefinitely unless a shorter period is specified, subject to applicable statutes of limitations or repose.

In **Section 8.1, Survival; Exclusive Remedy** [62] the parties agreed that the representations and warranties would survive the closing and continue as

---

[19]   This express survival clause is included in the asset purchase agreement to avoid the possibility that a court might apply the common law principle that representations merge with the sale of assets and therefore cannot form the basis of a remedy after closing. Even under the common law approach, however, warranties survive closing and will support strict liability recovery until the applicable statute of limitations runs out.

long as WKH was making royalty payments to iCare, which would extend to April 1, 2016. However, the parties also agreed that the following representations and warranties would survive indefinitely:

- Organization and Good Standing, found in **Sections 4.1** [61] **and 5.1** [67]

- Authorization of Agreement, found in **Sections 4.2** [61] **and 5.2** [67]

- Conflicts; Consents, found in **Sections 4.3** [61] **and 5.3** [67]

- Assets of the Business, found in **Section 4.9** [61]

- Financial Advisors, found in **Section 5.5** [67]

- Transactions with Affiliates, found in **Section 4.23** [61]

Representations and warranties pertaining to Taxes, Section 4.8 [61]; Employee Benefit Plans, Section 4.12 [61]; and Environmental Matters would last until the expiration of the relevant statute of limitations.[20] Those representations and warranties pertaining to intellectual property [61] were to last

---

[20] Because states generally do not permit parties to contractually extend the statute of limitations, the portions of the survival clause providing longer or indefinite survival periods may be unenforceable to the extent they have the survival period extend beyond the statute of limitations for breach of contract claims.

five years after closing.[21] In the event that either party provided written notice of a claim for an inaccuracy during the survival period, the claim would survive beyond the period until it was finally resolved.

Although the inaccuracy of a representation that survives the closing may form the basis for a claim of breach of the APA without an indemnification provision, it is customary for such agreements to contain a clearly specified right to indemnification for breaches of representations, warranties, covenants, agreements, and other obligations. The **Obligations of Seller to Indemnify** [62] provision found in **Section 8.2** [62], mirrors the corresponding provision **Obligations of the Buyer to Indemnify**, **Section 8.3** [62]. In essence, both parties agree to indemnify each other for misrepresentations that lead to any losses incurred by the parties.

Section 8.4, Notice and Opportunity to Defend [62] provides various procedures the parties must follow with respect to third party claims. It deals primarily with notice requirements and the control of legal proceedings. Because the purchasing company is the indemnified party in most circumstances, it is more concerned with the indemnified party's rights under this provision. iCare is mainly concerned with the indemnifying party's rights. This provision also requires the indemnified party to provide the indemnifying party with written notice of a third party claim within 30 days after the

---

[21]   The parties agreed that five years would be the useful product life of the software.

indemnifying party receives notice. It also provides the indemnifying party with the right to assume the defense of such third party claim. In the event that the indemnified party provides the defense of such claims, it requires cooperation of the indemnifying party in the defense of the claim. In the event that there was an Approved Indemnification Claim, the parties agreed to make payments to the indemnified party by wire transfer within 5 days.

Indemnification was one of the more heavily negotiated provisions between iCare and WKH. The members of iCare clearly did not want any personal exposure, nor did they want to accept any responsibility for indemnification beyond the purchase price being paid for the iCare product. WKH made two major concessions as documented in **Sections 8.5 Limitations of Liability and 8.6 Recourse Only to Seller** [62]. WKH agreed to limit iCare's indemnification obligations to a threshold amount of $25,000 and an indemnity cap of $100,000,[22] unless iCare breached one of the following provisions:

---

[22]   These limitation provisions are often referred to as "Baskets" and "Caps". A basket provides that an indemnifying party is not liable for inaccuracies in or breaches of certain representations until a specified minimum dollar amount is exceeded. The basket in Section 8.5 is structured as a threshold, which provides that iCare is liable for the total amount of losses only once the minimum amount of $25,000 is exceeded (also referred to as "tipping" basket). The cap of $100,000 provides a ceiling on indemnification for representations and warranties, subject to certain exceptions agreed to by the buyer.

- **Section 8.5(c) Buyer's Right of Offset** [62]

- **Section 4.10 Seller's Representations and Warranties regarding the Intellectual Property** [61]

- **Section 6.3 Non-Competition; Non-Solicitation** [68]

- **Section 6.4 Confidentiality** [68]

- **Section 8.2(e)** [62] any fraud, intentional misrepresentation, or criminal acts committed by or on behalf of iCare or any affiliate on or prior to the closing with respect to this agreement, the business, the acquired assets or the acquired intellectual property

- **Section 8.2(f)** [62] the excluded assets or the excluded liabilities, except to the extent caused by the failure of a representation or warranty of buyer under this agreement to be true and correct.

These limits on liability meant that iCare would only be liable for losses once a threshold amount of $25,000 was exceeded, but also that once the threshold amount was reached, iCare would be liable for the full amount up to the indemnity cap of $100,000. However, if the breach pertained to any of the above listed provisions, the indemnity would also extend to include all future payments and royalties due iCare, because of WKH's right to offset. However, the recourse-only-to-the-seller provision limited recovery to only iCare LLC, blocking any recovery from the individual members. Although the liability limitations inherent in the LLC structure would also prevent recovery from the individual members, this provision added an additional, contractual level of assurance that recovery would not be sought outside the limits of the purchase price. While these provisions seemed ominous to the iCare members, the student attorneys assured them that they were included as a routine matter to limit the buyer's risk in the transaction and would hopefully never be resorted to.

X. ARTICLE IX—MISCELLANEOUS [74]

The miscellaneous article is also commonly referred to as "General Provisions" or "Boilerplate" which are standard provisions included in almost every transactional document. While the term "miscellaneous" is used by the drafter of this agreement, it should not reflect negatively on its legal import, as these provisions often trigger important, fundamental issues in contract law. These provisions typically come into effect when there is a problem or disagreement between the parties, so they must be carefully considered to ensure that they work correctly when they are needed most. The Miscellaneous Article in this transaction contained the following provisions:

- **Section 9.1 Payment of Sales, Use or Similar Taxes** [74]—In most states with sales taxes, whenever assets are being sold, the sales tax will apply to the receipts from the sold assets unless the assets sold are for resale by the buyer. In each state, it is important to determine the applicability of the sales tax, its exceptions, and on which party falls the duty of payment, collection, and remittance to the state. Notwithstanding the seller's legal duties of payment and collection of sale's taxes, how the sales tax payment obligation will be satisfied can be negotiated between the parties. In this transaction, iCare accepted the responsibility to pay all taxes imposed as a result of or associated with the transaction.

- **Section 9.2 Audit Rights** [74]—Because iCare was to receive future payments in the form of royalties for the sale of the iCare product in the market place, it wanted to have a right to check to see if they were being accurately compensated. Because an audit can be both disruptive to normal operations and costly, the negotiations of this provision centered on notice, timing, and on how the costs of the audit should be allocated between the parties. The parties ended up agreeing to limit audits to once a year, and only within a 90-day period after royalties were paid. Furthermore, iCare would pay for the audit by an independent accounting firm (acceptable to WKH and subject to its confidentiality agreement). In the event of underpayments of more than 5%, WKH would reimburse iCare for that amount plus the cost of the audit. If royalties were overpaid, iCare would reimburse the purchasing company.

- **Section 9.3 Expenses** [74]—In the absence of a specific agreement to the contrary, the costs and expenses of negotiating, drafting, and performing an agreement are paid by the party incurring the costs. This provision clearly sets out the party's intention that each side of the transaction pay its own costs associated with the transaction. The only exceptions to this provision are found in Section 9.1 and 9.2. [74], where the parties have agreed that iCare would pay sales or similar taxes associated with the transaction and both parties would be responsible for the cost of an audit based on the defined criteria.

- **Section 9.4 Entire Agreement; Amendments and Waivers** [74]—This provision combines three standard clauses. The entire agreement clause (also known as the merger or integration clause) is used to prevent the parties from being bound by or liable for any understandings or agreements other than those expressly set out in the asset purchase agreement and any other transaction documents—essentially it is intended to trigger the application of the parol evidence rule. The amendment clause precludes a party from arguing that there is an oral agreement to modify any of the agreement's terms or conditions. The waiver clause prevents a non-compliant party from arguing that the other party waived its rights under the agreement because it excused the non-compliance on an

earlier occasion or delayed or failed to exercise
their contractual rights.

- **Section 9.5 Notices** [74]—This provision
  governs the manner in which any notice under
  the asset purchase agreement must be given,
  and the time at which the notice is deemed to
  be received. The traditional means of giving
  notice was through the U.S. postal service,
  however, giving notice and sending other
  communications by hand, overnight courier,
  and facsimile are also acceptable. Note that
  notice by e-mail is not included in this
  provision. This was intentional as e-mail was
  deemed too easy to overlook or accidentally
  delete by the affected parties.

- **Section 9.6 Severability** [74]—The purpose
  of the severability clause is to clarify that, if
  one or more terms or provisions are held to be
  invalid, illegal, or unenforceable, the parties
  intend the asset purchase agreement to
  survive by severing the invalid, illegal, or
  unenforceable terms or provisions from the
  agreement.

- **Section 9.7 Binding Effect; Assignment;
  Third Party Beneficiaries** [74]—This
  section requires the other party's consent
  before a party may assign its rights under the
  asset purchase agreement, except that WKH
  may assign its rights, obligations, and
  interests to an affiliate, subsidiary, or third
  party. Other exceptions are contemplated in
  Article VIII [62], where payments can be paid

to third parties who are subject to the indemnification provision, or Section 2.3(i) [41], where the University of Tennessee and the college of nursing are the third party beneficiaries of a royalty-free, non-transferable license to use the most recent iCare product.

- **Section 9.8. Counterparts** [59]—This clause permits the agreement to be executed in multiple, identical copies when, for example, the parties do not sign the same physical document in the same location. However, it does require that the documents be identical; and arguably the execution of a signature page alone does not constitute an agreement between the parties. The counterpart clause makes it clear that each party need not sign the same physical copy of the document in order to have a legally enforceable agreement. In the iCare transaction, a virtual closing was conducted (the principal parties were located in Chicago, Illinois, and Knoxville, Tennessee). The signature pages of each document associated with the asset sales agreement were signed by the parties and sent via e-mail to WKH's counsel in Chicago to close the transaction.

- **Section 9.9 Waiver of Jury Trial** [74]— This provision is frequently included in agreements between sophisticated parties when drafting complex agreements because they would rather have a judge hear and decide any dispute rather than have people who may not fully appreciate and understand the potentially complex issues involved in the litigation. The clause used in the iCare Asset Purchase Agreement also specifically included that the waiver pertains to any other documents of the buyer or the seller that became a part of the transaction, as well as any cause of action arising out of the transaction.[23]

- **Section 9.10 Governing Law** [74]—This section permits the parties to select the law that governs the asset purchase agreement and the jurisdiction and venue in which a claim can be brought. (Sometimes designation of jurisdiction and venue are included in a separate "Choice of Forum" provision) Most agreements provide for both federal and state jurisdiction. In this instance, WKH, which is headquartered in Chicago, Illinois, chose the substantive law of the state of Illinois to govern the terms of the agreement and the state and federal courts located in Chicago,

---

[23] Contract provisions waiving a jury trial are valid and enforceable in most states. Generally state courts have enforced these provisions if: (1) the waiver is knowing and voluntary; (2) the waiver is clear and unambiguous; and (3) there is no adequate basis to deny enforcing the waiver, such as an allegation of fraudulent inducement of either the waiver itself or the contract as a whole. Because state laws vary on the exact standards for enforcing a jury waiver clause, parties should be familiar with the specific state laws governing their transaction.

Illinois, to have exclusive jurisdiction over any claims brought based on the agreement.[24]

- **Section 9.11 Specific Performance** [74]— It was important to WKH that iCare perform its obligations rather than simply being liable for damages on default. For example, it was critical that the confidentiality, non-competition, and non-solicitation covenants be specifically adhered to. The value of the iCare product in the market place could be compromised if competitors were provided certain confidential information or the iCare members competed with or solicited business from potential purchasing company clients. In addition, as part of the purchase price, the members of iCare agreed to perform work under the Master Consulting Agreement [51] to assist in the transition of the iCare product to the purchasing company and to assist with future enhancements to the product. Including a specific performance provision in the agreement (acknowledging the purchasing company's right to seek specific performance or an injunction to prevent breaches of confidentiality or non-competition) were essential to this transaction.

---

[24] In general, parties should choose the law of a state that has a relationship to the parties or the transaction. Parties may also consider other factors, such as which state has more favorable substantive laws applicable to the matters covered by the agreement.

- ## Section 9.12 Informal Dispute Resolution

  [74]—Many agreements contain an Alternative Dispute Resolution (ADR) provision. ADR is an informal process by which the parties to a dispute meet with a neutral third party, either in mediation or arbitration, who assists the parties in settling the dispute.[25] In this agreement, the parties employ a fairly progressive informal dispute resolution provision that outlines the process for resolving disputes between the parties by designating two principal negotiators who were the two primary business people who were responsible for reaching the agreement. This sort of dispute resolution is particularly attractive when, as here, a long-term working relationship between the parties is contemplated. Since it was the business people who actually worked out the basic business terms of the agreement, they are in the best position to recall and have flexibility to resolve disputes over matters that were

---

[25]   Mediation is perhaps the most relaxed and informal of ADR proceedings. During a mediation, the mediator in his or her role as a mediator will work to facilitate communication between the parties, identify and reframe the issues, and break the stalemate that has prevented the case from settling prior to the mediation. In arbitration, the parties to a dispute present their arguments and evidence to an impartial arbitrator who will render an award for one side. Arbitration can either be a legally binding proceeding that is non-appealable or it can be a non-binding proceeding. Unlike mediation, arbitration is a more formal proceeding, with less control in the client's hands. It looks like a somewhat informal version of a trial, conducted by a private arbitrator rather than a government judge.

perhaps not anticipated by the parties during negotiations.

QUESTIONS

1. What is the purpose of an asset purchase agreement (APA)?

2. What are the advantages of being the party who takes the lead in drafting the APA?

3. Which Article was the heart of the iCare APA? Why?

4. How were schedules used in Article II of the iCare APA?

5. What definitions in Article I were important in Article II, section 2.3 "Purchase Price Royalties" [49]?

6. What effect would bundling the iCare product have on the payment of royalties?

7. How were the iCare founders' concerns regarding their obligations to consult with addressed?

8. What were iCare and UTRF's concerns regarding the University of Tennessee's "Use Rights" that were proposed in the LOI?

9. How was this concern addressed?

10. What are Representations and Warranties and what is their purpose in an agreement?

11. What is the purpose of covenants in the APA?

12. Did iCare have to change or cease using its name under the APA? If yes, under what provision(s)?

13. Why were the iCare members concerned regarding the indemnification provisions?

14. How were their concerns addressed?

15. Which of the provisions in Article IX—Miscellaneous are most important? Why?

CHAPTER 7

SALE OF THE BUSINESS: FINALIZING THE TRANSACTION

I. THE CLOSING NOTEBOOK

Once the parties went through the process of negotiating, drafting, and marking-up the asset purchase agreement or APA, WKH's outside counsel prepared a "Closing Notebook." The Closing Notebook contains not only the Asset Purchase Agreement itself, but the schedules referenced in the agreement, along with all of the ancillary documents that effectively transfered all of the assets and agreed upon liabilities to the purchasing company. All of these documents were compiled, tabbed and identified at the beginning of the notebook in a Closing Index [75].

Schedules and Exhibits are used and referenced within the Asset Purchase Agreement to make it more readable. For example, rather than including the excluded liabilities in **Section 2.2 Assumed and Excluded Liabilities** [47], they are referenced in the that section and listed in **Schedule 2.2(b)** [48]. Schedules are also valuable for detailed explanations and procedures necessary to resolve operational issues that can be contemplated in advance. For example, **Section 2.3 Purchase Price; Royalties** [49] explains in detail how and when the royalty portion of the purchase price will be paid, but the detailed explanation of how the royalties will be calculated and the parameters under which they will be reduced are set out in **Schedule 2.3(h)** [53].

The same is true with the exhibits that follow the schedules. When listing the **Closing Deliveries of Seller in Section 7.1** [58], rather than including the ancillary contracts which effectively transfer the assets to the purchasing company within the body of the asset purchase agreement, they are included as exhibits to the agreement following the schedules.

The APA itself is not usually sufficient to transfer the assets to the purchasing company.[1] The APA merely provides that at closing the seller will transfer the assets being acquired to the buyer, and the buyer will assume certain specified liabilities from the seller. Asset purchase agreements are meant to be executed and delivered prior to the time of closing and are not intended to convey assets and liabilities to the buyer. The documents contained in the exhibits—generally called "instruments"—actually transfer ownership of the assets. Even where the signing of the APA occurs simultaneously with the transfer of assets (as was the case with iCare), it is preferable to convey title to assets in separate documents so that if proof of ownership needs to be shown to third parties or recorded on public records, it can be done so without providing the entire asset purchase agreement. In the iCare transaction, the

---

[1]   This is in contrast to a stock purchase agreement where no documents are necessary to transfer specific assets of the business being purchased to the buyer. When the stock is transferred to the new buyer, the corporation's assets remain property of the corporation, which now has a new shareholder or shareholders.

four founders, Wyatt [72], Bell [88], Li [89], and Indrandoi [90], each individually assigned all of their rights to the iCare IP to WKH.

II. THE CLOSING

In the iCare transaction, all of the documents were prepared, reviewed and finalized prior to closing. As mentioned in the previous chapter, this was a virtual closing as the parties to the transaction were located in Chicago, Illinois, and Knoxville, Tennessee. The participants at closing included the individual members of iCare (including the University of Tennessee Research Foundation (UTRF) and their outside counsel), WKH's president/CEO and her in-house counsel, WKH's outside counsel, and the student attorneys representing iCare, all of which met via teleconference. WKH's outside counsel led the discussion and took the parties through the agreement, article by article, specifically discussing those items that were heavily negotiated and how those issues were satisfactorily resolved between the parties.

Where required, the individual iCare members signed the signature pages of the documents relinquishing their individual interests in the intellectual property through the **Assignments of Intellectual** Property [72, 88, 89, 90] and acknowledging their participation in on-going developmental obligations as part of the **Master Consulting Services Agreement** [51]. In addition, the iCare officers signed the **Officers Certificate of iCare Academic, Limited Liability Company**

[76], certifying that iCare is an organization in good standing with the Tennessee Secretary of State at the time of the asset sale, as well as an **Action Taken By Written Consent by the Members of iCare Academic, LLC** [21],[2] authorizing the sale of its assets to the WKH. A similar authorization was signed by the directors of the WKH.

Tami Wyatt as President of iCare and the President of UTRF signed the **Amended and Restated Basic Agreement** [31], establishing the fact that iCare had licensing rights in all the enhancements that were made to the EHR system since they received the initial rights in the technology earlier in the year.[3] The amendment was necessary to make it clear that iCare had all the rights in the now existing version of the EHR system that it was now conveying to WKH. Wyatt and UTRF's president also signed a **Side Agreement** [77] which acknowledged the sale of the assets of the company,

---

[2] In the Operating Agreement of iCare Academic Limited Liability Company [8], Section 9.3 (Actions Taken Without a Meeting) allows the board of directors of the LLC to consent to an action without holding a meeting. Where a directors' meeting or shareholders' meeting cannot be held, the same matter can be authorized by an Action Taken by Written Consent that is signed by all of the directors or shareholders as the case may be.

[3] As you will recall from Chapter 3, the Basic Agreement officially assigns the rights in the technology from the university to UTRF, and it sets out the financial relationship among the inventors (e.g., should revenues be obtained, how the royalties will be split between the inventors and the university). The purpose of the Amended and Restated Basic Agreement was to acknowledge that there were a number of enhancements made to the EHR system since the first Basic Agreement was entered into on August 17, 2010, and to recognize that these enhancements were included in the license agreement that iCare had with UTRF.

reserving rights for perpetual, royalty-free use of the technology for the university and placing responsibility on the inventors for the payment of the university's share of the income from the sale. In turn, the **Asset Purchase Agreement** [71], dated December 1, 2010, was then signed by Wyatt and the president and CEO of the purchasing company. Once the signature pages for all of these documents were signed,[4] they were scanned and exchanged via e-mail between the parties.

Simultaneously with the execution of the APA, WKH transferred $300,000 to iCare's bank account, which was the capped amount of reimbursement for the development and operating costs related to the iCare product set out in **Section 2.3 Purchase Price; Royalties** [49] and **Schedule 2.3(a)** [50]. These actions fulfilled the requirements contained in **Article VII—Closing Deliveries** [58], finalizing the transaction.

III. POST-CLOSING ACTIVITIES

Once the APA and supporting documents that effectively conveyed title to the assets being purchased were signed, the parties now had to perform the mutual obligations contained in the asset purchase agreement. These obligations came primarily from **Article II—Purchase and Sale of**

---

[4]   The ability to have the documents to the assets purchase transaction signed in this fashion is authorized by **Section 9.8 Counterparts.** [59] This clause permits the agreement to be executed in multiple, identical copies when, for example, the parties do not sign the document in the same location.

Assets [41], **Article V—Representations and Warranties** [67], and **Article VI—Covenants** [68].

iCare was responsible for making commercially reasonable efforts to:

- Transfer all of the intellectual property pertaining to the iCare product;

- Provide ongoing development assistance outlined in the Master Consulting Agreement [51];

- Cooperate in the allocation of purchase price and preparation of tax returns for purposes of consistency of reporting;

- Transfer all material contracts;

- Cooperate in the defense in the event of any future litigation pertaining to the iCare product;

- Maintain the confidentiality of all iCare and WKH proprietary information;

- Refrain from competing with WKH or soliciting business with WKH's customers;

- Discontinue the use of the word iCare in any form; and

- Provide ongoing assistance in responding to accounting, financial, and tax reporting for the six-year period for which royalties are paid.

WKH was responsible for making commercially reasonable efforts to:

- Pay $500,000 by wire transfer to iCare's designated bank account by January 31, 2011;

- Pay 2011 royalties by wire transfer to iCare's designated bank account by April 1, 2012;

- Pay 2012 the Guarantee Amount royalties by wire transfer to iCare's designated bank account by February 15, 2013, and any excess royalties by April 1, 2013;

- Pay 2013 the Guarantee Amount royalties by wire transfer to iCare's designated bank account by February 15, 2014, and any excess royalties by April 1, 2014;

- Pay 2014 the Guarantee Amount royalties by wire transfer to iCare's designated bank account by February 15, 2015, and any excess royalties by April 1, 2015;

- Pay 2015 royalties by wire transfer to iCare's designated bank account by April 1, 2016;

- Cooperate in the allocation of purchase price and preparation of tax returns for purposes of consistency of reporting; and

- Cooperate in the defense in the event of any future litigation pertaining to the iCare product.

In addition to the obligations identified above, iCare had the additional reporting and payment obligations to UTRF, as outlined in the **Side Agreement** [77].

IV. THE STATUS OF iCARE ACADEMIC LLC GOING FORWARD

After the assets were transferred from iCare Academic Limited Liability Company, there was nothing left of value in the entity. Although the individual members wanted to continue working together on other projects and had ongoing individual responsibilities to both WKH and UTRF, they did not know whether they should or needed to maintain the limited liability company. In addition, while they were working with their accountant in coordinating the allocation of the asset purchase price from WKH, the accountant discussed the tax consequences of the asset sale to the membership. While the members recognized that distributions made from iCare Academic LLC's sale of the assets would be taxed as income on their individual federal tax returns,[5] they had not realized that the entity itself would be subject to state excise and franchise taxes.[6]

---

[5]   Recall that LLCs that elect to be taxed as partnerships do not pay income taxes at the business level. Any business income or loss is "passed-through" to owners and reported on their personal federal income tax returns. Any tax due is paid at the individual level.

[6]   The State of Tennessee imposes two taxes for the privilege of doing business within its boundaries. These taxes are the excise tax and the franchise tax and they are imposed on corporations and most limited liability companies. General partnerships and sole proprietorships are not subject to these taxes. The excise tax is based on the net income of the company for the tax year. The franchise tax is an asset based tax on the greater of net worth of the company or the book value of real and tangible personal property owned or used in Tennessee at the end of the taxable period.

The iCare members consulted the student attorneys to discuss these issues and determine the appropriate course of action. They were advised that at a minimum they needed to change the name of the LLC, removing the word "iCare" to comply with the requirements of the asset purchase agreement. However, concerns about pending state tax issues led the student attorneys to suggest that the existing LLC be dissolved and a general partnership formed. Much like an LLC, partners report the partnership profit or loss on their individual income tax returns. Although operating as a general partnership would be without the liability protection that the LLC provided,[7] future royalty payments would not be subject to state franchise and excise taxes. Given the limited amount of risk of liability that the members would be exposed to after the asset sale, they decided to dissolve iCare Academic LLC, form a partnership,

---

The **excise** tax is a 6.5% tax on the net earnings from business done in Tennessee for the year. Net earnings (and losses) are defined as federal taxable income (or loss), before the net operating loss deduction and special deductions provided for in the Internal Revenue Code, plus or minus certain additions or deductions as required by state law. The **franchise** tax rate is 25 cents per $100, or major fraction thereof, applied to the greater of a taxpayer's net worth or the book value of property owned or used in Tennessee at the close of the tax year covered by the required return. The minimum franchise tax payable each year is $100. Even if your business is inactive or has had its charter or other registration forfeited, but has not been legally dissolved, it is not relieved from filing a return and paying the minimum franchise tax.

[7]   The distinguishing feature of a partnership is the *unlimited liability* of the partners. Each partner is personally liable for all of the debts of the partnership. That includes any debts incurred by any of the other partners on behalf of the partnership. Any one partner is able to bind the partnership by entering into a contract on behalf of the partnership.

and purchase insurance to cover any reasonable risks.

V. DISSOLVING ICARE LLC

Officially ending iCare Academic LLC's existence as a state-registered business entity and, by extension, putting it beyond the reach of creditors, begins with a formal process called "dissolution." In order to voluntarily dissolve iCare Academic LLC, the student attorneys first looked at iCare's formational documents—the articles of organization [2] and operating agreement [8].[8] The operating agreement allowed for dissolution by majority vote of the members. As a result, an Action Taken By Written Consent [21] was drafted, and signed by all of the iCare's members.[9]

Once the membership gave approval, a Notice of Dissolution was filed with the Tennessee Secretary of State's Division of Business Services. The notice of dissolution contains the following basic information:

---

[8]   The Operating Agreement of iCare Academic Limited Liability Company, Article XVIII (Dissolution and Winding Up) [91], provided the process that the members agreed to take when they formed the entity.

[9]   In the event that the articles of organization or operating agreement did not contain dissolution provisions, the process would be governed by Tennessee's Limited Liability Company Act which requires a majority vote of the membership and defines how much advance notice members need of the meeting to vote and what information the meeting notice must contain.

- the name of the LLC;

- the date of the meeting at which the resolution to dissolve was approved, and a statement that the requisite vote of the members was received, or that members validly took action without a meeting; and

- the effective date for the notice if other than the filing date (not later than 90 days after filing).[10]

Once the membership vote has been taken and a Notice of Dissolution [78] filed, the company continues to exist only for the purpose of taking care of certain final matters that, collectively, are known as "winding up" the company. Under Tennessee's LLC Act, key winding up tasks include:

- collecting or making provision for the collection of all known debts due or owing to the LLC, including unperformed contribution agreements;

- paying or making provision for the payment of all known debts, obligations, and liabilities of the LLC;

- selling, leasing, transferring, or otherwise disposing of all or substantially all of the LLC's property and assets; and

---

[10]   There is a $20 fee to file the Notice of Dissolution (Form SS-4246). The filing will usually be processed within 3–5 business days. You may also receive same-day processing if you deliver the notice in person.

- distributing any remaining property, including money, to LLC members.

Section 18.3 of Operating Agreement [91] required that all creditors be paid first, including LLC members who were creditors. While providing notice to creditors can be very time consuming and drag out the wind up process, it does help limit liability and also allows safer, more final distributions to members. And, although not required, providing notice does provide protection for individual members, as they may be personally liable for those debts if notice is not given.

Fortunately, in this instance the only outstanding creditors were the members who originally loaned money to the company through promissory notes during the start-up period, and the deferred compensation owed to Harry King and Rich Berube as contactors to iCare. These creditors were paid with the initial deposit of $500,000 made by WKH on January 31, 2011. Once these creditors were paid, the accountant calculated the amount of state franchise and excise taxes that were owed to the Tennessee Department of Revenue and paid that obligation. The remaining money in the bank account was then distributed to the members based upon their percentage of membership interest. After dissolving and winding up the company, the student attorneys filed Articles of Termination [79] with the Secretary of State's Division of Business Services. These Articles of Termination included:

- the name of the LLC
- the date of filing of the LLC's articles of organization
- the reason for filing the articles of termination (a member vote to dissolve in accordance with the operating agreement); and
- an indication of whether known and potential creditors and claimants have been notified of the dissolution.

Once the Articles of Termination were processed by the Secretary of State, iCare Academic Limited Liability Company was dissolved.

VI. CREATING AND OPERATING AS A GENERAL PARTNERSHIP

Once iCare Academic Limited Liability Company's existence was terminated, the members decided on a new name for the partnership and the student attorneys drafted the Partnership Agreement of Academic Technology Innovations [80]. Much like the operating agreement for an LLC, a partnership agreement is not a mandatory legal requirement for establishing a partnership. However, it is a very important step to ensure that there are no misunderstandings between the partners. A well-drafted partnership agreement will help partners decide in advance how to handle certain situations. After the former iCare Academic LLC members reviewed and signed the agreement they began operating as a partnership.

The partners obtained a new IRS employer identification number and established a new bank account for the partnership. The partnership provided notice of these changes both to the WKH and UTRF. The partnership continues to perform the contractual obligations that iCare Academic LLC entered into with both the WKH and UTRF, only under a different entity structure.

QUESTIONS

1. What is a Closing Notebook?

2. How did the closing occur in the iCare transaction?

3. Did the closing conclude the transaction?

4. What happened to iCare Academic LLC after the closing?

5. How was this accomplished?

CONCLUSION

The purpose of this book has been to take you through the basic business and legal steps involved with forming a company, licensing technology, developing that technology, and harvesting or monetizing the assets that the business created through a sale of substantially all of the company's assets, and winding up the business. Hopefully, it has demystified the process involved. Although iCare was a short-lived company, all the transactions described here and the transactional documents and instruments involved in this transaction are applicable to deals involving companies as large as Google (Alphabet), Apple Computer, Berkshire Hathaway, and Amgen Pharmaceuticals. We hope that this discussion and presentation has piqued your interest in business lawyering, especially as 75% or more of practicing lawyers in the United States are not primarily courtroom lawyers or litigators but, rather, function as business deal or regulatory attorneys, and many find it very fulfilling to serve in the role of trusted advisor to their clients as they navigate the seas of business and commerce.